Table of Contents

Chapter 04:Delicious, Quick, And Easy Breakfast Millet 65

Chapter 05: Delicious, Quick, and Easy Lunch Recipes 86

Special Bonus!

Want This Bonus Challenge + Book for FREE?

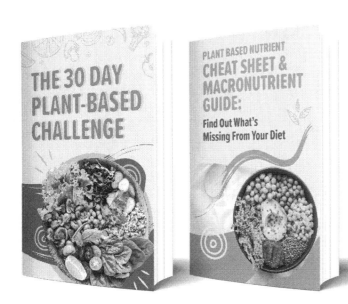

Get FREE, unlimited access to it and all of my new books by joining the Fan Base!

Scan W/ Your Camera To Join!

Before we get started, I'd like to offer you this gift. It's my way of saying thank you for spending time with me in this book. Your gift is a special report titled *"The 30-Day Plant-Based Challenge."* As a bonus, you will also receive *"The Plant-Based Nutrient Cheat Sheet & Micronutrient Guide."* This is a 30-day challenge, and an easy-to-use guide that pulls together tons of analysis and fun activities you can enjoy doing every day. This guide will help you understand what exactly could be missing in your plant-based diet to achieve your health and fitness dreams. This guide will make sure you are eating clean and making sure you are getting all the nutrients you need daily to help you along with whatever fitness dreams you have. Whether you want to lose weight, burn fat, build lean muscle, or even bump up your confidence, this challenge and guide are just for you.

Paulgreencookbook.com

This 2 in 1 gift includes:

✓ <u>Complete 30 days</u> of daily plant-based fun and activities you will love

✓ <u>80+ detailed micronutrient information</u> of the most common plant-based foods at your fingertips

✓ <u>Basic Beginner steps</u> to cover all the basic information you need to hop into the plant-based lifestyle

✓ The micronutrient guide will provide you with <u>essential information</u> about the body's vitamin and mineral requirements

✓ The <u>cheat sheet guide</u> will make your transition to a whole foods plant-based diet very simple

I'm willing to bet you'll find at least a few ideas, tools and meals covered in this gift that will surprise and help you. This guide will set you up for success and is a proven system when starting your plant-based journey. With this guide, you will be armed with the info & focus you need. You will be giving your body nutritious fuel and enjoy eating plant-based foods. With downloading this guide, you're taking a solid step to the path of your health and fitness dreams.

How can you obtain a copy of **The 30-Day Plant-Based Challenge** and the **Plant-Based Nutrient Cheat Sheet & Micronutrient Guide?** It's simple. Visit paulgreencookbook.com and sign up for my email list (or simply click the link above). You'll receive immediate access to the guides in PDF format. You can read it online, download it or print it out. Everything you need to get started and stay on your plant-based journey is included when you sign up for my email list.

Being on my email list also means you'll be the first to know when I release a new book. I plan to release my books at a steep discount (or even for free). By signing up for my email list, you'll get an early notification.

If you don't want to join my list, that's fine. This just means I need to earn your trust. With this in mind, I think you will love the information I've included in the ultimate guide. More specifically, I think you will love what it can do for your life.

Without further ado, let's jump into this book.

Join The Plant-Based Health, Fitness, And Nutrition Facebook Group

Looking for a community of like minded individuals who love all things plant based, working out, fitness, nutrition and health? If so, then check out my Facebook community: The Plant-Based, Health, Fitness and Nutrition Community.

This is an amazing group of plant-based health enthusiasts who focus on getting results with their lives. Here you can discover simple strategies along your health journey, build powerful habits and relationships, find accountability partners, and ask questions about your struggles. I also host free book giveaways and share other helpful free resources that will be the key to reaching your health and fitness goals as fast as possible. If you want to "level up" in your health and fitness journey then this is the place to be.

**Just scan the QR code below
to join The Plant-Based, Health, Fitness and Nutrition Community**

Attention

Do Not Turn The Page Until You Have Read Everything Below

Scan the QR code below to receive the colored ebook version of this cookbook!

Scan W/ Camera Now!

Due to printing costs, we are not able to provide you with a print book with colors and pictures. Instead, I have provided you the ebook version for you to download completely for free with the full cookbook for your ultimate plant-based experience. I want my book to be easily accessible for everyone in the world and since we are a small publishing company, this is the best we can offer to still keep the price for you as low as possible. Hopefully, in the near future, we would like to change this by offering the best quality of books in the world for the lowest prices. Thank you for your understanding and we greatly appreciate your support.

Introduction

"An estimated 99 percent of people who have a problem with eating gluten don't even know it. They ascribe their ill health or symptoms to something else – not gluten sensitivity – which is 100 percent curable."
–Dr. Mark Hyman

Dr. Mark Hyman's quote from his article Gluten: What You Don't Know Might Kill You, fits perfectly as an opening to this gluten-free vegan cookbook. There are few dangers to human health as widespread as the unknown consequences of consuming gluten.

The symptoms of gluten resistance are all too often confused with other health conditions. This can lead to misdiagnosis and a lack of treatment. If left unchecked, and if the warning signs go unheeded, these side effects of consuming the seemingly ever-present structural protein can have a profoundly negative effect on our lives. Gluten intolerance can lead to excessive fatigue, anxiety, depression, bloating, indigestion, weight loss, and even chronic skin conditions.

Gluten resistance and intolerance can be caused by a variety of factors. Once it is recognized, it can be treated by maintaining a gluten-free diet. If you have discovered that you have celiac disease, non-celiac gluten sensitivity, a wheat allergy, or even suspect that you suffer from any of these conditions despite not being diagnosed, this cookbook will be an invaluable tool in the journey to improving your health.

I was already a vegan when I first discovered that I had gluten sensitivities. Depending on the recipe, I'd experience bloating, nausea, and fatigue. Having already cut out animal-based products, I was at a loss as to what was causing those ailments. It was my understanding that a healthier diet would be enough. That's when I realized that many vegan foods still contained gluten so I sought a way to eliminate the structural protein from my meals.

The transition from a purely vegan diet to one bereft of gluten wasn't simple. One of the main hurdles was that many plant-based ingredients were rich in hidden gluten. After extensive research, I could compile a diverse cookbook full of vegan, gluten-free recipes. All of them were designed to be cooked in thirty minutes. That makes them ideal for integrating into even the busiest of schedules.

It is my sincere hope that you experience the same benefits I did after switching to a gluten-free, vegan diet. Contained within these pages is everything you need to know to about gluten, gluten resistance, the challenges of the affliction, and how to work around it. There are quick and easy-to-make recipes designed for every meal of the day. We even cover healthy snacks and treats, which are ideal for satiating those mid-day cravings. I've even included tips for helping friends and/or family who might be suffering from gluten intolerance as well. So, what are we waiting for? Let's get started!

CHAPTER 01

GLUTEN RESISTANCE

What Is Gluten Resistance? The Science

The simplest definition of gluten resistance refers to the body's inability to digest gluten proteins. There's a wide range of symptoms attached to this condition that aren't merely confined to the digestive system. It's important to remember that if you experience any of the symptoms listed in this book, you should consult a doctor to receive a proper diagnosis before beginning any kind of treatment for it.

What does gluten do?

One of the most misunderstood nutrients commonly found in food, gluten is a group of proteins known as "prolamins". Some foods contain more of these prolamins, such as wheat, rye, and barley. Those proteins, especially those found in wheat (gliadin and lutenin), cannot be fully broken down by the digestive enzymes in the human gastrointestinal (GI) tract. This is partially due to the amino acids in gluten called "proline" and "peptides".

Prolines and peptides pass through the wall of the small intestines and spread to other parts of the body. Once out of the GI tract, these amino acids cause inflammatory and immunological responses in those who have gluten sensitivities.

The main difference between those with gluten resistance and those who do not is how their bodies' immune systems respond to the proliferation of amino acids. That also leads to a wide variety of responses as no two people's immune systems are the same.

 Types of gluten intolerance

Gluten resistance can occur due to different reasons, and each type of sensitivity brings out different symptoms. Here are some common forms of gluten resistance. If you experience any of these it's important to get yourself looked at by a medical professional.

— Celiac disease

Celiac disease is an auto-immune condition that flares up upon the ingestion of gluten. The proteins destroy the internal lining of the small intestine, which can have very serious effects on the whole body. Symptoms of celiac include diarrhea, bloating, and abdominal pain.

Long-term gluten intake, without treatment, can cause more serious symptoms in the afflicted. Their bone mineral density can decrease. Celiac patients can suffer considerable weight loss, iron deficiencies (anemia), muscle weakness, and even seizures.

The worldwide prevalence of celiac disease varies. Some nations have higher rates than others. According to the experts, about one to two percent of Americans suffer from the condition. It is more prevalent among women. Hereditary, environmental, and other autoimmune conditions are all factors in developing celiac. Most doctors agree that rigorous adherence to a gluten-free diet is key to controlling the symptoms and managing the disease.

— Wheat allergy

The proteins found in wheat can cause allergic reactions in those with wheat allergies. Although this can affect adults, it's significantly more common in teens and children. When someone with wheat allergies ingests these proteins, it can cause a spectrum of reactions but the most dangerous is potentially fatal anaphylaxis.

The 30-Minute Gluten-free Vegan Cookbook for Beginners
150 simple, delicious, and nutritious whole food, plant-based, and Gluten-free recipes. Make them in under 30 minutes to improve your health and lose weight

15

— Non-celiac gluten sensitivity

Gluten sensitivities aren't restricted to just celiac disease and wheat allergies. Some people without those conditions still react negatively to the group of proteins. This is called, "Non-celiac gluten sensitivity" (NCGS).

Though the cause of NCGS is disputed among researchers, most agree that its symptoms are related to a patient's immune response. As such, it's much more likely to occur in those who already have autoimmune diseases. Doctors must eliminate celiac and wheat allergies through proper evaluation and testing before diagnosing someone with NCGS.

Research done in 2019 found that NCGS is substantially more prevalent than celiac disease and according to some estimations could affect up to thirteen percent of the human population. Like celiac disease, it's more prevalent among women than men. In addition to gastrointestinal symptoms such as bloating and diarrhea, NCGS sufferers can experience fatigue, anxiety, and headaches. Relief for patients can be found in strictly cutting gluten from their diet.

16

The 30-Minute Gluten-free Vegan Cookbook for Beginners
150 simple, delicious, and nutritious whole food, plant-based, and Gluten-free recipes. Make them in under 30 minutes to improve your health and lose weight

Challenges of Being Gluten Resistant

Each type of gluten resistance presents its own set of challenges. All of them are a legitimate threat to your health. However, the reactions of each variety are unique. To counter those negative symptoms, we first have to identify which form of gluten resistance you have and how to fashion a diet around it.

Challenges of celiac disease

— **Vomiting, diarrhea, and constipation**

When someone diagnosed with celiac disease consumes gluten, their small intestine becomes inflamed. That cascades into a litany of issues. Their gut lining gets damaged, which makes absorbing nutrients much harder and triggers diarrhea or constipation. Regular diarrhea can result in more complications, such as a loss of electrolytes, dehydration, and fatigue. One way to identify celiac as a possible diagnosis is if someone has pale and unpleasant-smelling stools – a result of poor nutritional absorption.

— **Fatigue**

Fatigue is one of the most prevalent symptoms of celiac disease. Several factors are believed to contribute to that exhaustion. An inability to get a restful night's sleep due to chronic pain and mental health conditions make sleeping harder. Anemia, a deficiency of iron in someone's blood that impairs the ability to generate healthy red blood cells, can also be caused by celiac disease leading to low energy and an overall sense of being worn out for sufferers.

The 30-Minute Gluten-free Vegan Cookbook for Beginners
150 simple, delicious, and nutritious whole food, plant-based, and Gluten-free recipes. Make them in under 30 minutes to improve your health and lose weight

17

— Skin reactions

Being diagnosed with celiac disease can lead to various skin conditions. Here is a short list of some of the skin disorders that can be caused by gluten intolerance:

- Psoriasis –scaling and reddening of the skin
- Alopecia areata – this autoimmune condition manifests as non-scarring hair loss
- Urticaria – recurrent itchy pink or red lesions with pale centers
- Dermatitis herpetiformis – causes blisters to form over the body

— Depression and anxiety

Like many chronic ailments, celiac disease can frequently lead to depression and anxiety. There are some theories on how these mental ailments can be exacerbated by gluten sensitivities. The production of the "happy hormone", serotonin, may be hampered by the condition which can lead to feelings of melancholy.

Peptides called "exorphins" are released when certain gluten proteins are digested. Those exorphins can disrupt the neural system, which could lead to an increased risk of depression in some people. The changes in a sufferer's intestinal microbiome can be a factor. The central nervous system may be negatively affected by higher levels of dangerous bacteria and lower levels of helpful bacteria in the digestive system. Too much of one and too little of the other can cascade into mental health issues.

— Unexplained weight loss

A sudden fluctuation in weight is always a legitimate matter of concern. Unexplained weight loss is frequently an indicator of celiac disease. Although there are several reasons why this occurs, the weight loss is normally tied to the lack of nutritional absorption, diarrhea, and constipation.

18

The 30-Minute Gluten-free Vegan Cookbook for Beginners
150 simple, delicious, and nutritious whole food, plant-based, and Gluten-free recipes. Make them in under 30 minutes to improve your health and lose weight

— Iron-deficiency anemia

Anemia is a common symptom in celiac patients. Identified via blood tests, anemia can have a litany of health risks associated with it. Some of the effects of the lack of iron include fatigue, headaches, dizziness, shortness of breath, weakness, and pale skin.

— Autoimmune disorders

Every time a celiac patient consumes gluten, it's an attack on their already compromised immune system. That can lead to all manner of further ailments. Celiac patients can become more likely to develop autoimmune thyroid disease, liver diseases, Type 1 diabetes, and inflammatory bowel disease.

— Joint and muscle pain

There are a couple of possible contributing factors to the joint and muscle pain celiac patients may experience. Anemia is one possible cause. There is another hypothesis that people with the condition have a neurological system that is genetically predisposed to being oversensitive or overexcited. That could explain their seemingly lower threshold for having sensory neurons triggered generating pain in a patient's muscles and joints.

The 30-Minute Gluten-free Vegan Cookbook for Beginners
150 simple, delicious, and nutritious whole food, plant-based, and Gluten-free recipes. Make them in under 30 minutes to improve your health and lose weight

19

🌿 Challenges of non-celiac gluten sensitivity (NCGS)

Despite being a milder form of gluten resistance and insensitivity, non-celiac gluten sensitivity can still cause serious life-altering symptoms. About 0.5-13% of the human population suffers from NCGS. They can experience any of all the associated challenges attached to the diagnosis.

— Digestive complications

Originating in a patient's gut, the symptoms of gluten sensitivities start in the digestive tract. The more common of these are bloating, constipation, diarrhea, and abdominal pain. Constipation affects roughly twenty-five percent of NCGS patients. Patients are about twice as likely to experience diarrhea consistently.

When someone with NCGS eats gluten-rich food, one of the first and most obvious symptoms is bloating. While compared to some of the other effects of the condition, bloating can seem relatively minor but it can lead to long periods of physical discomfort.

Abdominal pain is probably the most common symptom of NCGS. About eighty-three percent of people with gluten intolerance experience discomfort and pain after consuming the protein group. The severity varies but is a key contributor to the lower quality of life of those who aren't treated for the condition.

— Headaches

The negative effects of NCGS aren't limited to the digestive tract. Headaches and migraines are also prevalent among people with gluten intolerances. Be sure to get examined by a medical professional if you get frequent and unexplained headaches and/or migraines.

20

The 30-Minute Gluten-free Vegan Cookbook for Beginners
150 simple, delicious, and nutritious whole food, plant-based, and Gluten-free recipes. Make them in under 30 minutes to improve your health and lose weight

— Brain fog

Have you ever had trouble thinking clearly for no apparent reason? If you have, you've experienced brain fog. People who are gluten intolerant often have trouble concentrating, clouded thoughts, and a general feeling of mental weariness. Brain fog affects nearly forty percent of sufferers. No one knows for sure what causes this, but it might be a reaction to specific gluten-related antibodies.

The 30-Minute Gluten-free Vegan Cookbook for Beginners
150 simple, delicious, and nutritious whole food, plant-based, and Gluten-free recipes. Make them in under 30 minutes to improve your health and lose weight

21

🌿 Challenges of wheat allergy

Wheat allergies can lead to a litany of immune system responses when someone is exposed to the proteins found in gluten. More common in children than adults, wheat allergy gluten intolerance can lead to some of the more severe symptoms related to gluten resistance.

— Skin disorders

Generally one of the milder symptoms of wheat allergies, skin disorders can flare up due to exposure to gluten. Most of these rashes share some common characteristics such as itching, redness, and inflammation. There typically isn't much time between consuming gluten and the appearance of these disorders making the relationship between the two easier to identify. More severe reactions may need medical treatment.

— Nasal congestion

Other tell-tale symptoms of a wheat allergy are sneezing, nasal congestion, and a runny nose. Baker's asthma can develop from the repeated inhalation of bread flour, making said bakers more sensitive to the proteins found in wheat and other grains.

— Anaphylaxis

The most serious possible reaction to a wheat allergy is anaphylaxis. After exposure to the allergen, a sufferer can develop a variety of symptoms, including swelling, hives, nausea, vomiting, and difficulty breathing. A person's airways can even swell shut, leading to death if untreated. After the commencement of anaphylaxis, epinephrine needs to be injected directly into the skin to counter the reaction and possibly save the patient's life.

What It Takes to Switch to GF Foods

Our over-dependence on wheat and other gluten-rich products is so widespread that it can feel hard, if not impossible, to switch to a gluten-free lifestyle. The unfortunate truth is that there will have to be changes made in your everyday life. This is especially true when someone is first diagnosed as being gluten intolerant. However, the good news is that once you identify the problem, you can start your journey to better health.

Prepare your mind and your family

The first step to transitioning to a gluten-free lifestyle is accepting your situation. Eating gluten is bad for your health. To feel better, those foods need to be cut out. Once you're able to accept that, you can include your family and/or loved ones in your treatment. If your loved ones know about your gluten intolerance, they can accommodate you and give a helping hand down the road to a healthier diet.

Clean out your kitchen and pantry

Once diagnosed, it is time for a complete kitchen overhaul. Get rid of any gluten-rich products in your pantry, kitchen, and fridge. This is key to avoiding temptation and falling back into old eating habits. If you live with loved ones, a good compromise to ask them is to either keep their food in a separate cupboard, label gluten-rich foods or carve out a space of your own in the kitchen.

Start planning your meals

A good meal plan is the key to sticking to a diet. This is especially true if you have a restrictive diet like one that excludes gluten. Proper and careful planning can be the answer to all your health issues. This can help you avoid feeling overwhelmed.

Meal planning starts with grocery shopping. Think carefully about what you want to cook that week and what ingredients you need. It might be a good idea to clean your kitchen before heading out the door. Be sure to double-check labels while at the grocery store to ensure that you aren't consuming gluten proteins that will have adverse effects on your health.

The 30-Minute Gluten-free Vegan Cookbook for Beginners
150 simple, delicious, and nutritious whole food, plant-based, and Gluten-free recipes. Make them in under 30 minutes to improve your health and lose weight

23

Analyze food labels

If you didn't before, you must start reading the food labels of the products you buy at the grocery store. Gluten-free products have a certification or label printed on the packaging. Even a third-party gluten-free certification (such as the GFCO label) should be safe.

The safety of certified products comes from the regulations of the Food and Drug Administration (FDA). They demand that any food that claims to be gluten-free must have a gluten content of fewer than twenty parts per million (ppm) to qualify. These stringent qualifications aren't limited to the United States. In the European Union (EU), similar laws are in effect to protect customers with gluten intolerances.

Don't buy gluten-rich condiments

The sources of gluten in condiments and sauces are often hidden. Gluten can be added to condiments by food producers to serve as stabilizers, thickeners, or emulsifiers. The following condiments contain gluten and must be avoided or replaced with gluten-free alternatives:

- Barbecue sauce
- Malt vinegar
- Marinades
- Pasta sauce

- Salad dressing
- Soy sauce
- Teriyaki sauce
- Worcestershire sauce

It is beneficial to go over the allergies label on these condiments. Always keep in mind that a condiment may contain gluten from rye or barley as well, even if it doesn't contain any wheat. Take malt vinegar as an example; it contains gluten because it is made from barley. So, it must be avoided at all costs.

24

The 30-Minute Gluten-free Vegan Cookbook for Beginners
150 simple, delicious, and nutritious whole food, plant-based, and Gluten-free recipes. Make them in under 30 minutes to improve your health and lose weight

Beware of different types of wheat products

Reading food labels can be challenging because there are so many different types of wheat-sourced products, and each type is named differently. When examining a label for hidden sources of gluten, look for these names as well:

- Durum
- Einkorn
- Khorasan (Kamut)
- Spelt or farro
- Triticale
- Semolina
- Farina

In addition to these, common food additives like maltodextrin, caramel color, and modified food starch may contain undeclared sources of wheat and should also be avoided.

Explore more gluten-free alternatives

There are gluten-free alternatives for those with intolerances. Some of the most common are sorghum, teff, and buckwheat, which are gluten-free grains. Beans, salsa, guacamole, and corn tortillas are all safe to eat on this diet. Utilizing traditionally Indian ingredients such as lentils and cumin can add intense flavoring to your dishes. More than anything, this new diet allows exploring a wider range of ingredients and foods from around the world to flesh out and add variety to your dining options despite the restrictions.

The 30-Minute Gluten-free Vegan Cookbook for Beginners
150 simple, delicious, and nutritious whole food, plant-based, and Gluten-free recipes. Make them in under 30 minutes to improve your health and lose weight

25

Avoid cross-contact with gluten

Cross-contact (contamination) is one of the biggest culinary dangers when you're gluten intolerant. It often occurs when food is cooked or prepared on shared surfaces with kitchen tools that haven't been carefully cleaned after being used on gluten-rich ingredients. For example, kneading gluten-free dough over a wheat-floured surface would add gluten to your food. Toasters, sifters, and strainers can be risky if not properly and thoroughly washed. This is a major risk for people with celiac disease and especially wheat allergies. So be careful.

 ## Join a gluten-free community

The negative effects of gluten sensitivity aren't limited to physical reactions. Being on a strict gluten-free diet can feel isolating. Add to that the real risks of depression and melancholy associated with the different kinds of intolerance to the proteins and a sufferer can struggle with loneliness.

Luckily there is support for people who must live gluten-free. You can join the numerous online communities on message boards and social media. Plus, there's always the option of creating a community yourself connecting you with others who must live around this life-altering condition.

Being There for a Family Member Who Is Gluten-resistant

What does it mean for you if someone in your family and/or a loved one is diagnosed with a gluten-resistance? It means that you will play a part in their journey to better health. Whether you realize it or not, you can make a gigantic difference in improving their prospects. Here are some things you can do to help them while they struggle with this difficult and serious condition.

1 People with gluten intolerance tend to shy away from talking about their symptoms. There is a stigma attached to having a chronic condition. So, the least you can do for them is to listen. Having an outlet, someone to talk to about what's going on with their health can provide vital support, enabling them to stay on the path to better health.

2 Read more about gluten intolerance. The more knowledge you will have about the condition, the easier it will be for you to help your family. Remember that you can be a tool your loved one can utilize in their struggle.

3 Figuring out how to live with gluten intolerance is hard. It requires a massive change of lifestyle. There are things that you can do to help your loved one that will ease their new burden. You can help them prepare for their new gluten-free lifestyle by creating appropriate grocery lists, going to the store, and helping manage/organize their pantry.

4 Take your loved one to a health expert for dietary and lifestyle recommendations. Only an expert can diagnose the condition and offer treatment accordingly. Sometimes people can resist going to these professionals because they don't want to acknowledge their problems.

5 When planning to dine out, look for restaurants that offer meals with no gluten or help your loved one make a better choice by picking the right meals. It always helps to have an ally and advocate looking out for you.

6 You might want to consider joining your loved one on this journey. A vegan gluten-free lifestyle is guaranteed to be beneficial to your health as well. When you go down this path, you can share all the good and bad aspects of such a radical lifestyle change.

Basic Gluten-free Grains and Their Alternatives

Wheat, barley, rye, triticale, farina, spelt, Kamut, wheat berries, farro, and couscous are the ten different types of grains that contain gluten. They cannot be added to a gluten-free diet in any form. The good news is that you can replace these grains in your diet by adding the following alternatives:

 **Sorghum**

Typically, sorghum is grown for both animal feed and as a cereal grain. Along with several alcoholic beverages, it is also used to make sorghum syrup, a form of sweetener. This gluten-free grain has advantageous phytochemicals that work as antioxidants to lessen oxidative stress and lower your risk of developing chronic disease. Sorghum is also high in fiber, which can aid in reducing the rate at which sugar is absorbed into the body which helps maintain healthy blood sugar levels.

 **Quinoa**

One of the most consumed gluten-free grains nowadays is quinoa. It is very versatile and a wonderful source of plant-based protein and fiber. It's rich in antioxidants which can help the immune system and combat the negative effects of an autoimmune disorder. It is often difficult to obtain enough protein from a plant-based meal. Quinoa is one of the few options that are a complete protein source. Quinoa includes all eight of the essential amino acids that your body needs, unlike the majority of plant meals that are deficient in one or two of them. Quinoa flour can be used to make gluten-free crusts, casseroles, pancakes, tortillas, and fast bread. All of this makes it one of the most robust options in a vegan gluten-free diet.

(28)

The 30-Minute Gluten-free Vegan Cookbook for Beginners
150 simple, delicious, and nutritious whole food, plant-based, and Gluten-free recipes. Make them in under 30 minutes to improve your health and lose weight

Oats

One of the more abundant and affordable gluten-free grains is oats. It's also one of the top sources of beta-glucan, which is a soluble fiber that can reduce the amount of LDL (bad) cholesterol. It can be a vital part of your new diet. Beta-glucan can also decrease the absorption of sugar in the body, which lowers blood sugar and insulin levels – important for those with diabetes. Some celiac disease patients may be hyper-sensitive to one of the proteins in oats, avenin, so it's important to make sure that you can consume them. However, the vast majority of gluten-intolerant people can safely enjoy this beneficial grain.

 **Buckwheat**

Don't let buckwheat's name scare you off. It is a grain-like seed that is gluten-free and completely unrelated to traditional wheat. Like oats, it contains plenty of antioxidants such as rutin and quercetin. The former might lessen the symptoms of Alzheimer's disease. Buckwheat might also reduce the risks of heart disease.

 **Amaranth**

Amaranth was a dietary staple for past great civilizations like the Inca, Mayans, and Aztecs. The grain has amazing health benefits and is loaded with beneficial nutrients. Consuming amaranth can help reduce inflammation and reduce the risk of heart disease. It's also very malleable and can be used to replace couscous and other gluten-rich grains. When ground up, you can also use it as a substitute for cornstarch when thickening soups, jellies, and sauces.

 Teff

The smallest of all grains, Teff had an impressive nutritional profile. This is despite it being only a hundredth the size of a wheat kernel. It's packed with protein and meets a large portion of your daily fiber requirements. That means teff can be invaluable when looking to replace wheat flour for gluten-free baking.

The 30-Minute Gluten-free Vegan Cookbook for Beginners
150 simple, delicious, and nutritious whole food, plant-based, and Gluten-free recipes. Make them in under 30 minutes to improve your health and lose weight

29

Corn

Corn is one of the most widely consumed gluten-free cereal grains in the world. It's an excellent source of fiber. Corn is also rich in the plant proteins lutein and zeaxanthin. Both are carotenoids that act in much the same way as antioxidants. They can improve eye health, and lower the risk of developing cataracts and other forms of macular degeneration. Add to those benefits the sheer versatility of corn and it will become an integral part of your new diet.

Brown rice

Though you can eat all types of rice on a gluten-free diet, brown rice is the healthiest since it has more fiber and minerals. Both types of rice are gluten-free, however, research indicates that brown rice has more health benefits than white rice. Switching from white rice to brown can lower your risk of developing diabetes, weight gain, and heart disease.

30

The 30-Minute Gluten-free Vegan Cookbook for Beginners
150 simple, delicious, and nutritious whole food, plant-based, and Gluten-free recipes. Make them in under 30 minutes to improve your health and lose weight

Table: Gluten-free diet

In this table, you can find three categories of food, put together to simplify the changes to your diet. The first suggests a food that is rich in gluten and must be avoided altogether. The second column contains food that may contain a small amount of gluten due to cross-contamination. The last column has all the options that you can eat freely on a gluten-free diet.

Gluten-Rich Food to Avoid	Gluten Cross Contaminated Food to Avoid	What to Eat
Wheat	Fried foods	Beans and legumes
Spelt	Baking mixes	Fruits and vegetables
Kamut	Granola	Corn (corn flour, cornmeal, grits, polenta)
Triticale	Vegan protein bars	Rice (white rice, brown rice, basmati, etc.)
Durum	Multigrain chips	Amaranth
Einkorn	Soy sauce	Arrowroot powder
Farina	Artificial flavors	Buckwheat (kasha)
Semolina	Licorice and candy	Flaxseed
Cake flour	Creamy soups	Millet
Matzo	Salad dressings	Quinoa
Couscous	Seasonings	Sorghum
Barley	Beer	Tapioca
Malt	Malt liquor	Pure oats and oatmeal
Rye		Chickpea flour
Cereal		Coconut (coconut flour, oil, milk, etc.)
Cakes		Almonds (flour, milk, and seeds)
Cookies		Potatoes
Crackers		Vinegar and oils
Pretzels		Herbs and spices
Pasta		Baking powder and baking soda
Pizza crust		

The 30-Minute Gluten-free Vegan Cookbook for Beginners
150 simple, delicious, and nutritious whole food, plant-based, and Gluten-free recipes. Make them in under 30 minutes to improve your health and lose weight

31

CHAPTER 02

FINDING JOY WITH A VEGAN LIFESTYLE

Veganism is more than just a dietary approach. In many ways, it is a lifestyle, based on beliefs and principles. Not only does it have a spectrum of health benefits but it also takes our dietary choices' effects on the environment and ecosystem into consideration. When you become vegan, you take a pledge to avoid consuming every form of animal-sourced goods. Though it can seem like a highly restrictive lifestyle at first, it comes with significantly more positives than negatives. Not only does it improve your health, but it can also ease your conscience.

The 30-Minute Gluten-free Vegan Cookbook for Beginners
150 simple, delicious, and nutritious whole food, plant-based, and Gluten-free recipes. Make them in under 30 minutes to improve your health and lose weight

33

Benefits of a Vegan Diet

01. Offers a nutrient-dense diet

Healthy vegan diets are rich in nutritious whole foods such as fruits, vegetables, legumes, grains, nuts, and seeds. Unsurprisingly, several studies have found that vegans typically ingest higher amounts of fiber, antioxidants, potassium, magnesium, folate, and vitamins A, C, and E.

02. Reduces the risks of cancer and other diseases

Plant-based diets are dense with phytochemicals. Those phytochemicals have very potent antioxidants that can be found in fruit and vegetables. Researchers discovered that when compared to non-vegans, vegans consume higher amounts of unSaturated fatty acids, omega-3 fatty acids, and carotenoids. All of those are associated with better health and a decreased risk of cancer and chronic disease.

03. Vegan diet boosts your mood

A vegan lifestyle is a more compassionate lifestyle. There is no separating animal-based food products from cruelty and abuse. Some studies have proven that vegans, on average, are happier than those who consume meat. Compared to non-vegans, they score higher on depression tests and mood profiles. Plant-sourced antioxidants can even boost serotonin production in the body which means the improvement is more than mental, it's physical.

04. Maintains healthy body weight

Vegan meals typically contain fewer calories than those that include animal-sourced ingredients. That makes it easier to maintain a healthy weight without calorie counting. Quite a few studies state that vegans typically have lower body mass indices than non-vegans. This diet contains less saturated fat which helps keep the pounds off.

34

The 30-Minute Gluten-free Vegan Cookbook for Beginners
150 simple, delicious, and nutritious whole food, plant-based, and Gluten-free recipes. Make them in under 30 minutes to improve your health and lose weight

05. Prevents type-2 diabetes

Vegans may have up to seventy-eight percent less of a chance of developing type-2 diabetes. That is due to more controlled blood sugar levels and less consumption of saturated fatty acids and bad cholesterol.

06. Improves skin

The consumption of dairy is one of the most detrimental things you can do concerning the health of your skin. It's proven that eating or drinking dairy worsens acne in both men and women. Eating more vitamins and antioxidants adds more vitamins and antioxidants to your diet; vital for clearer skin.

07. Reduces the pain of arthritis

At its core, arthritis and its associated pain come from inflammation. A vegan diet introduces a whole host of antioxidants and phytonutrients that can reduce said inflammation. Probiotic plant-based foods like fermented vegetables contain live cultures that can increase good bacteria in the large intestine improving the health and balance of your digestive flora.

The 30-Minute Gluten-free Vegan Cookbook for Beginners
150 simple, delicious, and nutritious whole food, plant-based, and Gluten-free recipes. Make them in under 30 minutes to improve your health and lose weight

35

Do Vegans Live Longer?

A healthy diet combined with an active lifestyle gives you the best chance of fending off chronic disease and cancer. Adhering to both increases the likelihood of you living longer and healthier. Being vegan doesn't mean you'll age slower. It just means you will likely age well. You will feel younger and have more energy. On average, vegan males live ten years longer and women six years longer than their non-vegan counterparts.

36

The 30-Minute Gluten-free Vegan Cookbook for Beginners
150 simple, delicious, and nutritious whole food, plant-based, and Gluten-free recipes. Make them in under 30 minutes to improve your health and lose weight

Vegan Vs. Vegetarian

Veganism and vegetarianism are not the same thing. Many use the two terms interchangeably but the diets have considerable differences. Let's go over those differences to establish a clear understanding of the journey that lies ahead of you.

Vegetarianism is a diet

The main tenant of vegetarianism lies in the restriction of eating meats such as beef, pork, chicken, duck, turkey, shellfish, insects, and fish. That also includes byproducts sourced from the slaughter of animals such as rennet and gelatin. However, many vegetarians do consume animal-based products that do not include the killing of animals. They often still consume eggs and dairy products. Perhaps the biggest takeaway when thinking about the difference between a vegan and vegetarian diet is how much stricter the former is than the latter. Here are some genres of vegetarian diets:

— **Lacto-ovo-vegetarianism:** This diet forgoes all forms of meat and fish but includes eggs and dairy products in the meals.

— **Lacto-vegetarianism:** On this diet, people do not eat any meat, fish, or eggs but do consume dairy products.

— **Ovo-vegetarianism:** On this diet, people only eat eggs; they don't eat any meat, fish, or dairy products.

— **Pescatarian diet:** The only meats allowed on this diet are fish and other types of shellfish. The pescatarian diet is often referred to as semi-vegetarianism or flexitarianism because it does not conform to the conventional concept of vegetarianism.

The 30-Minute Gluten-free Vegan Cookbook for Beginners
150 simple, delicious, and nutritious whole food, plant-based and gluten-free recipes. Make them in under 30 minutes to improve your health and lose weight

37

❧ Veganism is a lifestyle

Veganism is the stricter version of vegetarianism, and there is no room for animal exploitation in this approach. Animal-sourced food or its byproducts are not consumed or used by vegans. According to the Vegan Society USA, being vegan means avoiding all forms of animal exploitation and cruelty, whether it be for the food industry, research, fashion, or any other reason. Any foods or drinks that contain any animal-sourced products are strictly forbidden for vegans, and that includes:

- Eggs, fish, poultry, and shellfish
- Dairy ingredients
- Honey

- Gelatin
- Rennet and other animal-derived proteins and lipids

Developing the Right Mentality to Go Vegan

The choices we make regarding what to eat are influenced by a variety of factors. Food availability and affordability are the most fundamental factors influencing how people choose to eat. But beyond that, people are influenced by a broad array of factors, such as personal tastes, social norms, convenience, and concerns about health, sustainability, and animal welfare. You can only make up your mind about following a certain restrictive lifestyle if you are mentally prepared for it. Staying vegan is more about how you see the world around you and what you think about your ecosystem. Unlike other dietary approaches, which are more goal-oriented and temporary, veganism is a lifelong commitment; it calls for developing the right mentality to adhere to it. Here are a few ways that will help you work on your mindset, as they did the same for me when I first opted for veganism.

❧ You are what you eat

There is a widespread axiom that says, "You are what you eat." Whatever you eat indirectly affects your emotions and your mental health. If you start thinking of food as something that affects your personality in the long run, you will start making better choices every day. On a vegan diet, you eat fiber-rich plants which contain essential phytonutrients responsible for rejuvenating your brain cells and improving your moods and emotions.

 38

The 30-Minute Gluten-free Vegan Cookbook for Beginners
150 simple, delicious, and nutritious whole food, plant-based, and Gluten-free recipes. Make them in under 30 minutes to improve your health and lose weight

🌿 Rethink animal cruelty

We all know that animal cruelty and killing innocent beings is unethical, but somehow we lose sight of this if it does not happen in front of us. To prepare your mind for the transition, you must visit the places where the animal-produced food is sourced from and rethink the damage of the dietary choices you make. By living on a vegan diet, you will not struggle with the ethical question of why you enjoy watching cows on pasture and then going out and eating a steak. Veganism makes interacting with animals more enjoyable because you will stop feeling guilty around animals.

🌿 Connect to your planet

Eating plants improves our health and is more environmentally friendly. It also makes us feel better to know that no living thing was harmed or killed to make our meal. By going vegan, you become more considerate of your environment. Once you start caring for the animals, you will also start standing up against other things that are destroying the planet's ecosystems.

🌿 One person can make the difference

Most people don't opt for veganism, thinking *what good can come out of one person changing his dietary habits?* But you must remember that every person and struggle is important, and together all the individuals make a large community of vegans who are proudly making a difference. It makes you confident to know that even as one person, you can influence change. Everyone has heard the argument that because the meat and dairy industries are so large, they won't even notice the loss of just one client; it doesn't matter when one person becomes a vegan. I can now state with confidence that it does matter. First, by being vegan, each of us may prevent the slaughter of at least 100 animals annually. For those animals, survival is important! Second, for the first time in history, meat consumption per person in America has been declining for several years.

The 30-Minute Gluten-free Vegan Cookbook for Beginners
150 simple, delicious, and nutritious whole food, plant-based, and Gluten-free recipes. Make them in under 30 minutes to improve your health and lose weight

39

Think about the health benefits

The most motivating factor in becoming vegan is the health benefits, which are thoroughly discussed in this chapter. What you need to do is to talk to the people around you who are following this approach and ask for their experience. Listening to their personal experiences and stories will greatly help you make up your mind.

Sustenance over exploitation

Being a vegan myself, my approach to looking at this lifestyle is a decision to choose sustenance without exploitation which means that to keep myself healthy, I don't need to harm other animals in the process because I can do so well by living on the plants. This way of thinking really helped me through my transition.

How to Enjoy Your Vegan Lifestyle

Though all the changes to your lifestyle may seem drastic, they don't mean life can't still be pleasurable. This is not a quick fifteen-day weight loss challenge. This is a lifelong commitment that will take time to adjust to. Once you do acclimate, you'll find that feeling better physically will lead to a considerably more enjoyable experience from day to day. Here are some techniques to help you enjoy your journey.

Start slowly

As stated above, going vegan isn't a quick fad diet. It's a lifestyle that might need to be eased into. Don't become discouraged if you need time to adjust. Figuring out the best pace for you is vital in committing to these changes.

One of the simplest ways to transition to a vegan diet is to do it slowly. Start with small adjustments. You can start by cutting out meat or dairy one day per week and work your way up from there. Or maybe you can have a vegan breakfast during the first week. From there you can have a vegan lunch the second week and build from there. I'd encourage you not to be afraid of experimentation. Try different vegan ingredients or substitutes. Finding a suitable alternative for your favorite foods is a good way to get your feet wet.

Do it right

Simply committing to a vegan diet doesn't mean that everything you eat will be inherently healthy. There are vegan versions of every type of junk food you can imagine. You will still have to plan a balanced diet packed with the vitamins and nutrients your body requires. This is especially true when you have to avoid gluten as well. That's why this authentic cookbook with tried and true recipes is a valuable resource. Let me be your guide in navigating around the pitfalls of trying to live healthily in a world that promotes the opposite.

The 30-Minute Gluten-free Vegan Cookbook for Beginners
150 simple, delicious, and nutritious whole food, plant-based, and Gluten-free recipes. Make them in under 30 minutes to improve your health and lose weight

41

Experiment to expand your menu

Variety is the spice of life. That idiom applies to your new gluten-free vegan diet as well. Instead of boring yourself with the same old salads and soups, try something new. The good news is that being vegan doesn't restrict you from exploring international cuisine, in fact, it encourages it. Experiment, and find what ingredients and flavors appeal to you. Enjoying the food you eat will help keep you on the right path.

Gain more knowledge

Even though I wrote this entire cookbook in addition to others on plant-based diets, I am still learning. I'm proud that despite all that I've compiled on my own journey, there is still much desire to learn. I would suggest you do the same. There is new research, strategies, and products out there to support not only vegans but those with gluten resistance. Do not shy away from the rapid changes that can keep your new lifestyle fun and interesting.

Focus on motivations

It's important to frequently remind yourself of the wide-ranging benefits of a vegan lifestyle. Remind yourself of the many advantages and how much better you feel than before. There will be days when it feels like too much work or you'll miss the foods from your old diet. That's when you need to take a deep breath and remember why you made the changes you did. Reading vegan-related literature or watching motivational videos can help. Maybe you can spend time with traditionally farmed animals to remind you of the very real cost of consuming intelligent living beings.

Stay consistent

Staying consistent with your diet is key. There might be failures or lapses in the beginning but the more you dedicate yourself to staying on the path, the easier it will become. What once took work will become a habit. Being vegan will start to feel natural.

42

The 30-Minute Gluten-free Vegan Cookbook for Beginners
150 simple, delicious, and nutritious whole food, plant-based, and Gluten-free recipes. Make them in under 30 minutes to improve your health and lose weight

Surround yourself with like-minded people

One of the key pieces of advice addicts in recovery receive from support systems is to stay away from other addicts. Being vegan is similar in that sense. Spending time with other vegans will help you stay the course. Connecting with others, especially online can also help you through periods of doubt or weakness. You are not alone.

Meal prep

Prepping your meals isn't necessary but if you have the time and energy, there are numerous benefits to doing so. Not the least of them is the trap of easy access to unhealthy junk food. If you always have meals ready and easily available, you'll be far more likely to make the right decisions when your stomach rumbles. The planning and discipline required to prep for a restrictive diet can provide benefits outside of the kitchen as well.

The 30-Minute Gluten-free Vegan Cookbook for Beginners
150 simple, delicious, and nutritious whole food, plant-based, and Gluten-free recipes. Make them in under 30 minutes to improve your health and lose weight

43

CHAPTER 03

DELICIOUS, QUICK, AND EASY SOUPS

Vegan Minestrone

Nutritional Values Per Serving	
Calories	385
Total Fat	2.3g
Saturated Fat	0.6g
Cholesterol	0mg
Sodium	799mg
Total Carbohydrate	66.6g
Dietary Fiber	14g
Total Sugars	4.2g
Protein	26.1g

 Servings
6

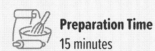 **Preparation Time**
15 minutes

 Cooking Time
18 minutes

Ingredients:

- 2 tablespoons water
- ½ white onion, diced
- 3 garlic cloves, minced
- 2 large carrots, peeled and sliced
- 1½ cups green beans, chopped
- ¼ teaspoon sea salt
- ¼ teaspoon black pepper
- 1 small zucchini, sliced
- 1 (15-ounce) can diced fire-roasted tomatoes

- 6 cups vegetable broth
- 2 teaspoons dried basil
- 2 teaspoons dried oregano
- 1 tablespoon nutritional yeast
- 1 pinch red chili pepper flake
- 1 tablespoon coconut sugar
- 1 (15-ounce) can white beans
- 2 cups shirataki noodles
- 1 cup kale, shredded

Instructions:

1. Place a large Dutch oven over medium heat and add water, onion, and garlic.
2. Sauté this mixture for 3 minutes, then add carrots, green beans, salt, and black pepper.
3. Sauté for 4 minutes, then add tomatoes, broth, zucchini, basil, oregano, yeast, red pepper flakes, beans, and coconut sugar.
4. Cook this mixture for 12 minutes on medium-high heat with occasional stirring.
5. Add kale and shirataki noodles then cook for 3 minutes.
6. Garnish with herbs and vegan cheese.
7. Serve warm.

Storage Tips:

Pour the soup into a sealable container and refrigerate for no more than 2 days or freeze it for up to 3 months. Reheat the soup over medium-low heat to serve again.

The 30-Minute Gluten-free Vegan Cookbook for Beginners
150 simple, delicious, and nutritious whole food, plant-based, and Gluten-free recipes. Make them in under 30 minutes to improve your health and lose weight

45

Vegetable Soup

 Servings
6

 Preparation Time
10 minutes

 Cooking Time
13 minutes

Nutritional Values Per Serving	
Calories	169
Total Fat	2.4g
Saturated Fat	0.6g
Cholesterol	0mg
Sodium	1456mg
Total Carbohydrate	28.5g
Dietary Fiber	6.5g
Total Sugars	8.5g
Protein	9.6g

Ingredients:

- 2 tablespoons avocado oil
- 2 cups onion, diced
- 2 tablespoons garlic, chopped
- 3 cups frozen mixed veggies
- 1 potato, chopped into bite-size pieces
- 1 (14-ounce) can of stewed tomatoes
- 1 (14-ounce) can diced tomatoes
- 3 cups zucchini, diced
- 6 cups vegetable broth
- 1 teaspoon granulated garlic
- ½ sprig rosemary
- 2 tablespoon parsley, chopped
- 1 teaspoon thyme
- 1½ teaspoons salt
- ½ teaspoon black pepper
- 2 bay leaves

Instructions:

1. Add onion, garlic, and oil to your Instant Pot and sauté for 3 minutes on Sauté mode.
2. Stir in potato, veggies, zucchini, broth, tomatoes, and all seasonings.
3. Put on its pressure cooking lid and cook on high pressure for 10 minutes
4. Naturally release the pressure from the Instant Pot and remove the lid.
5. Garnish with parsley.
6. Serve warm.

Storage Tips:

You can store the soup in a food-grade ziplock plastic bag. Place the bag in a container with its mouth open and pour the soup into it. Remove the air and seal the bag. Refrigerate for no more than 3 days or freeze it for up to 3 months.

Lentil Soup

Nutritional Values Per Serving

Calories	368
Total Fat	14.5g
Saturated Fat	2.3g
Cholesterol	0mg
Sodium	1014 mg
Total Carbohydrate	47.6g
Dietary Fiber	10.2g
Total Sugars	8.1g
Protein	14.9g

 Servings 4

 Preparation Time 15 minutes

 Cooking Time 20 minutes

Ingredients:

- ¼ cup olive oil
- 1 medium onion, diced
- 3 celery stalks, diced
- 2 carrots, diced
- 3 garlic cloves, minced
- 3 small Yukon gold potatoes, diced
- 1 teaspoon dried thyme
- ½ teaspoon dried oregano
- ¼ teaspoon smoked paprika
- 1 (15-ounce) can diced fire-roasted tomatoes
- 4 cups vegetable broth
- 2 bay leaves
- 2 cups water
- 1¼ cups orange lentils, rinsed and picked over
- 2 tablespoons red wine vinegar
- ¼ cup parsley, chopped
- Salt and black pepper, to taste

Instructions:

1. Add oil, onion, garlic, celery, carrot, salt, and black pepper to your Instant Pot.
2. Sauté the veggies on Sauté mode for 5 minutes.
3. Stir in potatoes and the rest of the ingredients.
4. Put on the pressure cooking lid, seal the pot and cook for 15 minutes on high pressure.
5. Once done, release the pressure of the cooker completely, then remove the lid.
6. Garnish and serve warm.

Serving Suggestion:

Enjoy this soup with a cucumber and tomato salad.

Storage Tips:

This lentil soup can be best stored in a freezer, and to do so, pack it in a small ziplock bag or reaction-free container.

The 30-Minute Gluten-free Vegan Cookbook for Beginners
150 simple, delicious, and nutritious whole food, plant-based, and Gluten-free recipes. Make them in under 30 minutes to improve your health and lose weight

47

Mushroom Soup

Nutritional Values Per Serving	
Calories	335
Total Fat	32g
Saturated Fat	22.1g
Cholesterol	0mg
Sodium	60 1mg
Total Carbohydrate	14.8g
Dietary Fiber	3.8g
Total Sugars	8.6g
Protein	6.7g

 Servings 4

 Preparation Time 15 minutes

 Cooking Time 25 minutes

Ingredients:

- 2 tablespoons olive oil
- 1 sweet onion diced
- 4 garlic cloves, minced
- 16 ounces of mushrooms, sliced
- ¼ teaspoon Himalayan sea salt
- 1 teaspoon Herbes de Provence
- ⅓ cup almond flour
- 3 cups vegetable stock
- 1 (13-ounce) can of coconut milk
- Salt and black pepper to taste

Instructions:

1. Add onion, garlic, and oil to a cooking pot and sauté for 5 minutes.
2. Stir in Himalayan sea salt, mushrooms, and Herbes de Provence, then cook for 10 minutes
3. Add almond flour and mix well with the mushrooms.
4. Pour in coconut milk and stock, then cook for 10 minutes on medium-high heat.
5. Stir in black pepper, salt, and thyme.
6. Serve warm.

Serving Suggestion:

Serve this mushroom soup with a fresh kale salad on the side.

Storage Tips:

Pack the soup in a sealable container and store it for no more than 2 days in the refrigerator for storage. Reheat on low heat before serving.

Carrot and Sweet Potato Soup

Nutritional Values Per Serving	
Calories	306
Total Fat	20.7g
Saturated Fat	18.3g
Cholesterol	0mg
Sodium	1778mg
Total Carbohydrate	32.5g
Dietary Fiber	7.5g
Total Sugars	15.1g
Protein	4.5g

 Servings
3

 Preparation Time
10 minutes

Cooking Time
15 minutes

Ingredients:

- 1 medium sweet potato, peeled and diced
- 1 pound carrots, peeled and sliced
- 1 small yellow onion, chopped
- 3 garlic cloves, sliced
- 2 cups vegetable stock
- 1 cup water

- 1 tablespoon ginger root, minced
- 1 ½ teaspoons dried dill
- 1 ½ teaspoons salt
- ½ teaspoon dried thyme
- ½ teaspoon ground nutmeg
- 1 cup almond milk

Instructions:

1. Add stock, water, carrots, sweet potato, and the rest of the ingredients to a cooking pot.
2. Cook for 15 minutes on medium-high heat until veggies are soft.
3. Puree this soup with a hand blender until smooth.
4. Serve warm.

Serving Suggestion:

Serve this soup with freshly made cucumber salad.

Storage Tips:

Pack the soup in a food-grade ziplock bag, flatten this bag and freeze for up to 3 months. Let the soup freeze for 24 hours before stacking other soup packets on top.

The 30-Minute Gluten-free Vegan Cookbook for Beginners
150 simple, delicious, and nutritious whole food, plant-based, and Gluten-free recipes. Make them in under 30 minutes to improve your health and lose weight

49

Creamy Broccoli Soup

 Servings
3

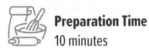 **Preparation Time**
10 minutes

 Cooking Time
19 minutes

Ingredients:

- 1 large broccoli head
- 1 potato, peeled and diced
- 1 white onion, diced
- 2 garlic cloves

- 2 cups vegetable stock
- 1 cup almond milk
- ½ cup water
- Salt and black pepper to taste

Instructions:

1. Add broccoli, potato, onion, garlic, stock, and water to an Instant Pot.
2. Put on the pressure cooking lid, seal the pot and cook for 8 minutes.
3. Once done, release the pressure naturally, then remove the lid.
4. Stir in almond milk, black pepper, and salt, then cook for 5 minutes.
5. Puree the soup with a blender until smooth.
6. Serve warm.

Serving Suggestion:

Serve this soup with roasted broccoli florets on top.

Storage Tips:

Pour the leftover soup into a sealable container, cover the lid and freeze for up to 3 months, or refrigerate for no more than 2 days.

The 30-Minute Gluten-free Vegan Cookbook for Beginners
150 simple, delicious, and nutritious whole food, plant-based, and Gluten-free recipes. Make them in under 30 minutes to improve your health and lose weight

Tomato Soup

Nutritional Values Per Serving	
Calories	193
Total Fat	8.5g
Saturated Fat	2.4g
Cholesterol	0mg
Sodium	710mg
Total Carbohydrate	30.2g
Dietary Fiber	5.2g
Total Sugars	7.3g
Protein	3.6g

 Servings 2

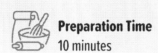 **Preparation Time** 10 minutes

 **Cooking Time** 17 minutes

Ingredients:

- 1 tablespoon olive oil
- ½ cup diced onion
- 1 stick celery, chopped
- 1 medium carrot, chopped
- 1 garlic clove, chopped
- 1 (28-ounce) tin diced tomatoes

- 1 medium potato, peeled and diced
- 1 ½ cups vegetable stock
- 2 teaspoons salt
- 1 teaspoon dried parsley
- 1 teaspoon granulated sugar
- ½ teaspoon ground black pepper

Instructions:

1. Sauté onion, garlic, carrot, and celery with oil in an Instant Pot for 10 minutes on sauté mode.
2. Stir in the rest of the ingredients and put on the pressure lid.
3. Seal the pot and cook for 7 minutes under high pressure.
4. Once done, release the pressure completely, then remove the lid.
5. Puree the cooked soup with an immersion or hand blender until smooth.
6. Serve hot.

Storage Tips:

Keep this soup stored in your refrigerator for no more than 2 days or freeze for a longer storage time.

The 30-Minute Gluten-free Vegan Cookbook for Beginners
150 simple, delicious, and nutritious whole food, plant-based, and Gluten-free recipes. Make them in under 30 minutes to improve your health and lose weight

51

Eggplant Soup

Nutritional Values Per Serving	
Calories	350
Total Fat	17.6g
Saturated Fat	2.9g
Cholesterol	0mg
Sodium	786mg
Total Carbohydrate	39.3g
Dietary Fiber	19g
Total Sugars	19.7g
Protein	15.5g

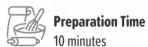 **Servings**
4

 Preparation Time
10 minutes

Cooking Time
25 minutes

Ingredients:

- 4 medium eggplant, peeled and halved
- 2 red bell peppers, halved
- 1 red onion, chopped
- 3 garlic cloves, minced
- 2 tablespoons olive oil

- 4 cups vegetable broth
- ¼ cup or 2 tablespoons tahini
- 1 teaspoon curry powder
- 1 teaspoon garam masala
- 1 teaspoon chili powder

Instructions:

1. Preheat your oven to 500 degrees F.
2. Line a baking sheet with an aluminum sheet and grease it with nonstick spray.
3. Spread eggplant and bell peppers on the baking sheet and roast for 20 minutes.
4. Sauté onion with oil in a skillet for 5 minutes, then stir in garlic.

5. Sauté for 30 seconds and add broth, spices, tahini, and roasted veggies.
6. Puree the cooked soup with an immersion or hand blender until smooth.
7. Serve warm.

Serving Suggestion:

Enjoy the soup with a bowl of cucumber salad on the side.

Storage Tips:

This eggplant soup can be best stored in a freezer, and to do so, pack it in a small ziplock bag or reaction-free container.

52

The 30-Minute Gluten-free Vegan Cookbook for Beginners
150 simple, delicious, and nutritious whole food, plant-based, and Gluten-free recipes. Make them in under 30 minutes to improve your health and lose weight

Vegan Clam Chowder

Nutritional Values Per Serving	
Calories	306
Total Fat	4.6g
Saturated Fat	0.8g
Cholesterol	0mg
Sodium	706mg
Total Carbohydrate	57.3g
Dietary Fiber	9.1g
Total Sugars	5.9g
Protein	8.4g

 Servings
6

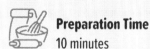 **Preparation Time**
10 minutes

 Cooking Time
28 minutes

Ingredients:

Mushroom Clam

- ½ cup shiitake mushrooms, chopped
- ¼ cup white wine
- ½ teaspoon celery seed
- 1 teaspoon vegan butter

Cream Sauce

- 1 cup cauliflower, lightly steamed
- ¾ cup almond milk
- 1 tablespoon almond butter
- ¼ teaspoon salt
- ¼ teaspoon cracked black pepper

Soup Base

- ½ medium yellow onion
- 2 celery stalks, rinsed, chopped
- 3 medium-sized carrots, chopped
- ⅓ cup frozen corn
- 1 teaspoon dried thyme
- 3 tablespoon almond flour
- 1 medium potato, cubed
- 3 cups vegetable broth
- ½ cup almond milk
- ¼ cup fresh parsley, chopped

Instructions:

1. Add mushrooms and butter to a cooking pot and sauté for 5 minutes.
2. Stir in celery seeds and white wine, then mix well and transfer to a plate.
3. Blend the cream sauce ingredients in a blender until smooth.
4. Sauté onions with celery, corn, carrots, and thyme in a skillet for 5 minutes.
5. Add the almond flour and mix well.
6. Stir in milk, broth, and potatoes, then cook for 15 minutes.
7. Add the sauteed mushrooms and cream sauce then cook for 3 minutes.
8. Garnish with parsley and serve warm.

Storage Tips:

To preserve the flavors, store the soup in your refrigerator for no more than 48 hours or freeze it in a food-grade zip lock bag for up to 3 months.

The 30-Minute Gluten-free Vegan Cookbook for Beginners
150 simple, delicious, and nutritious whole food, plant-based, and Gluten-free recipes. Make them in under 30 minutes to improve your health and lose weight

53

Rosemary White Bean Soup

Nutritional Values Per Serving

Calories	348
Total Fat	4.4g
Saturated Fat	0.8g
Cholesterol	0mg
Sodium	896mg
Total Carbohydrate	60.9g
Dietary Fiber	18.4g
Total Sugars	6g
Protein	18.5g

Servings
6

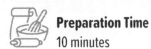 **Preparation Time**
10 minutes

 **Cooking Time**
27 minutes

Ingredients:

- 1 tablespoon olive oil
- 1 small sweet onion, chopped
- 3 celery stalks, chopped
- 2 carrots, peeled and chopped
- 1 (30 ounces) canned white beans Great Northern beans
- 1 can (32-ounce) vegetable broth
- 3 potatoes, peeled and diced
- 3 teaspoons fresh rosemary, chopped
- ½ teaspoon salt
- ¼ teaspoon black pepper

Instructions:

1. Add oil, celery, onion, and carrots to a soup pot and cook for 7 minutes on medium-high heat.
2. Stir in beans, broth, potatoes, rosemary, black pepper, and salt, then cook to a boil.
3. Cook the soup on high heat for 15 minutes, then puree with a hand blender.
4. Serve warm.

Storage Tips:

This pureed white soup is best stored in a freezer, and to do so, pack it in a small ziplock bag or reaction-free container.

Cauliflower Sweet Potato Soup

Nutritional Values Per Serving	
Calories	173
Total Fat	2.9g
Saturated Fat	2.1g
Cholesterol	0mg
Sodium	853mg
Total Carbohydrate	36.3g
Dietary Fiber	11.9g
Total Sugars	14.7g
Protein	8.5g

 Servings
4

 Preparation Time
10 minutes

Cooking Time
26 minutes

Ingredients:

- 1 large white onion, diced
- 4 garlic cloves, peeled and minced
- 1 tablespoon curry powder
- 1 teaspoon red pepper flakes
- 1 (14-ounce) can of coconut milk
- 4 cups vegetable stock
- 1 large sweet potato, peeled and cubed
- 1 medium head of cauliflower, chopped
- 2 tablespoons fresh lime juice
- 1 tablespoon organic cane sugar
- 1 cup green peas, fresh

Instructions:

1. Add onions, garlic, and 2 tablespoons of stock to a soup pot and cook for 6 minutes.
2. Stir in curry powder, red pepper flakes, stock, coconut milk, sweet potato, sugar, lime, and cauliflower.
3. Cover and cook the soup for 20 minutes.
4. Puree the cooked soup with an immersion or handheld blender.
5. Stir in green peas, black pepper, and salt.
6. Garnish with cilantro and lime juice.
7. Serve warm.

Serving Suggestion:

Serve with roasted cauliflower florets on the side.

Storage Tips:

Transfer this cauliflower sweet potato soup to a food-grade plastic bag and vacuum seal it to store in your freezer.

The 30-Minute Gluten-free Vegan Cookbook for Beginners
150 simple, delicious, and nutritious whole food, plant-based, and Gluten-free recipes. Make them in under 30 minutes to improve your health and lose weight

55

Red Lentil Zucchini Soup

Nutritional Values Per Serving

Calories	382
Total Fat	8.6g
Saturated Fat	1.3g
Cholesterol	0mg
Sodium	45mg
Total Carbohydrate	58.1g
Dietary Fiber	26.7g
Total Sugars	8.4g
Protein	21.8g

 Servings
4

 Preparation Time
10 minutes

 Cooking Time
27 minutes

Ingredients:

- 2 tablespoon olive oil
- 1 medium onion, sliced
- 2 medium carrots, shredded
- 2 medium zucchini, peeled and diced
- 2 tomatoes, sliced
- 4 cups vegetable stock
- 2 cups water

- 1 ½ cups red lentils, rinsed
- 2 tablespoons red paprika
- 1 tablespoon garlic powder
- ½ teaspoon cayenne pepper
- Salt to taste
- Crushed red pepper to taste

Instructions:

1. Sauté onion with oil in a large pot for 4 minutes.
2. Stir in carrots and cook for 4 minutes.
3. Add tomatoes and zucchini, then cook for 4 minutes.
4. Stir in broth, lentils, water, red paprika, garlic powder, cayenne pepper, salt, and red pepper then cook to a boil.
5. Cover and cook for 15 minutes.
6. Serve warm.

Serving Suggestion:

Serve this soup with roasted potatoes on the side.

Storage Tips:

Do not store this soup in your refrigerator for more than 2 days. For the best taste, freeze it in a sealable container for up to 3 months.

Quinoa Sweet Potato Chowder

Nutritional Values Per Serving	
Calories	250
Total Fat	7.1g
Saturated Fat	1.2g
Cholesterol	0mg
Sodium	1034mg
Total Carbohydrate	37.7g
Dietary Fiber	4.8g
Total Sugars	5g
Protein	10.8g

 Servings 4

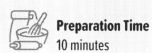 **Preparation Time** 10 minutes

 Cooking Time 25 minutes

Ingredients:

- 1 tablespoon olive oil
- 1 medium onion, chopped
- 1 large sweet potato, peeled and diced
- 32 ounces vegetable broth
- ⅔ cup quinoa
- 1 cup water
- ½ teaspoon garlic salt
- ½ teaspoon salt
- ½ teaspoon paprika
- ¼ teaspoon cumin
- ½ teaspoon white pepper
- 1 cup frozen corn
- Cilantro, chopped, to garnish

Instructions:

1. Sauté onion with oil in an Instant Pot on sauté mode for 5 minutes.
2. Add broth, quinoa, water, spices, and sweet potatoes, then cover with the pressure lid.
3. Seal the pot and cook for 15 minutes under high pressure.
4. Once done, release the pressure completely, then remove the lid.
5. Add corn and cook for 5 minutes.
6. Garnish with cilantro, then serve warm.

Serving Suggestion:

Serve this chowder with baked tofu skewers on the side.

Storage Tips:

Pour the leftover soup into a sealable container, cover the lid and freeze for up to 3 months or refrigerate for no more than 2 days.

The 30-Minute Gluten-free Vegan Cookbook for Beginners
150 simple, delicious, and nutritious whole food, plant-based, and Gluten-free recipes. Make them in under 30 minutes to improve your health and lose weight

57

Smoky Refried Bean Soup

Nutritional Values Per Serving	
Calories	429
Total Fat	4.8g
Saturated Fat	1.2g
Cholesterol	10mg
Sodium	1032mg
Total Carbohydrate	78.8g
Dietary Fiber	21.9g
Total Sugars	15g
Protein	24.2g

 Servings
2

 **Preparation Time**
5 minutes

 Cooking Time
26 minutes

Ingredients:

- 1 large onion chopped
- 3 garlic cloves, minced
- 1 green bell pepper, chopped
- 1 ½ cups vegetable broth
- 1 (14-ounce) can diced tomatoes
- 1 (15-ounce) can fat-free refried beans
- 1 (15-ounce) can cooked black beans

- 1 cup frozen corn kernels
- 1 teaspoon cumin
- 1 ½ teaspoons smoked paprika
- 1 teaspoon chipotle chili powder
- 1 teaspoon hot sauce or to taste
- ½ teaspoon Mexican oregano
- Salt and black pepper, to taste

Instructions:

1. Sauté onion in a stockpot with 2 tablespoons of broth for 5 minutes.
2. Stir in garlic and bell pepper then cook for 1 minute.
3. Add the rest of the ingredients and cook for 20 minutes.
4. Serve warm.

Serving Suggestion:

Add a dollop of vegan cream on top of the soup before serving.

Storage Tips:

Transfer this bean soup to a food-grade plastic bag and vacuum seal it to store in your freezer.

Vegan Cabbage Soup

Nutritional Values Per Serving

Calories	140
Total Fat	6.3g
Saturated Fat	1.1g
Cholesterol	0mg
Sodium	1003mg
Total Carbohydrate	14g
Dietary Fiber	4.3g
Total Sugars	6.1g
Protein	7.6g

 Servings 6

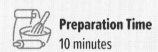 **Preparation Time** 10 minutes

 Cooking Time 28 minutes

Ingredients:

- 2 tablespoons olive oil
- 1 cup carrots, chopped
- 1 cup fennel, sliced
- ½ cup onion, chopped
- 2 teaspoons garlic, minced
- ½ teaspoon ground coriander
- ½ teaspoon salt
- 6 cups vegetable broth

- 1 (15-ounce) can of chopped tomatoes with herbs
- 1 (1 ½ lbs.) small head of green cabbage, chopped
- 1 (15-ounce) can of unsalted cannellini beans, rinsed
- 2 teaspoons sugar
- 1 teaspoon fresh oregano, chopped
- Lemon zest for garnish

Instructions:

1. Sauté carrots, onion, and fennel with oil in a soup pot for 5 minutes.
2. Stir in garlic, salt, and coriander, then cook for 1 minute.
3. Add tomatoes, broth, and cabbage, then cook on a simmer for 20 minutes.
4. Stir in beans, oregano, and sugar, then cook for 2 minutes.
5. Garnish with lemon zest and fennel fronds.
6. Serve warm.

Storage Tips:

To preserve the flavors, store the soup in your refrigerator for no more than 48 hours or freeze it in a food-grade zip lock bag for up to 3 months.

The 30-Minute Gluten-free Vegan Cookbook for Beginners
150 simple, delicious, and nutritious whole food, plant-based, and Gluten-free recipes. Make them in under 30 minutes to improve your health and lose weight

59

Pumpkin Black Bean Soup

Nutritional Values Per Serving

Calories	361
Total Fat	11.3g
Saturated Fat	1.9g
Cholesterol	0mg
Sodium	874mg
Total Carbohydrate	50.8g
Dietary Fiber	7.7g
Total Sugars	9.4g
Protein	16.9g

 Servings
4

 Preparation Time
5 minutes

 Cooking Time
20 minutes

Ingredients:

- 1 onion small, diced
- 1 cup vegetable broth
- 1 teaspoon curry powder
- 1 teaspoon cumin
- 2 teaspoons sea salt
- ¼ teaspoon cayenne powder
- Black pepper, to taste
- 2 cans (15-ounce) solid pumpkin

- 1 can (15.5-ounce) black bean chili beans, undrained
- 1 can (13.5-ounce) coconut milk
- 1 can (14.5-ounce) fire-roasted diced tomatoes, undrained

Toppings

- Pepitas and chopped chives

Instructions:

1. Add ½ cup broth and onion to a soup pan and cook for 10 minutes
2. Stir in the rest of the ingredients except the toppings and cook for 10 minutes
3. Garnish with pepitas and chives.
4. Serve warm.

Serving Suggestion:

Serve this soup with a bowl of your favorite kale salad.

Storage Tips:

This black bean soup is best stored in a freezer, and to do so, pack it in a small ziplock bag or reaction-free container.

Potato Soup

Nutritional Values Per Serving	
Calories	351
Total Fat	20.7g
Saturated Fat	17.2g
Cholesterol	0mg
Sodium	437mg
Total Carbohydrate	34g
Dietary Fiber	9.2g
Total Sugars	6.4g
Protein	12.9g

 Servings
6

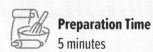 **Preparation Time**
5 minutes

 Cooking Time
26 minutes

Ingredients:

- 1½ lbs. potatoes, peeled and diced
- 3 celery stalks, chopped
- 3 carrots, chopped
- ½ medium yellow onion, chopped
- 4 garlic cloves, chopped
- 3 cups vegetable broth
- 2 cups almond milk
- ½ cup nutritional yeast
- 1 teaspoon dried thyme

- 1 teaspoon dried oregano
- 1 teaspoon dried parsley
- ½ teaspoon smoked paprika
- Salt to taste
- Cracked black pepper to taste

Garnish

- Diced green onion
- Vegan yogurt or sour cream

Instructions:

1. Sauté carrots, celery, and onion in a skillet for 5 minutes.
2. Stir in garlic, thyme, oregano, parsley, paprika, salt, and black pepper then cook for 1 minute.
3. Pour in milk and broth, then cook to a boil.
4. Add potatoes and cook for 10 minutes
5. Stir in yeast and mash the potatoes with a masher.
6. Garnish and serve warm.

Storage Tips:

Pack the soup in a food-grade ziplock bag, flatten this bag and freeze for no more than 3 months. Let the soup freeze for 24 hours before stacking other soup packets on top.

The 30-Minute Gluten-free Vegan Cookbook for Beginners
150 simple, delicious, and nutritious whole food, plant-based, and Gluten-free recipes. Make them in under 30 minutes to improve your health and lose weight

61

Coconut Curry Soup

Nutritional Values Per Serving	
Calories	261
Total Fat	14.1g
Saturated Fat	9.6g
Cholesterol	0mg
Sodium	1955mg
Total Carbohydrate	37.9g
Dietary Fiber	5g
Total Sugars	8.2g
Protein	7.7g

 Servings
4

 Preparation Time
10 minutes

 Cooking Time
28 minutes

Ingredients:

- 1 large sweet potato, spiralized
- 1 yellow onion, diced
- 3 garlic cloves, minced
- 1 tablespoon fresh ginger, minced
- 1 red bell pepper, julienned
- 2 tablespoons yellow curry powder
- 3 cups vegetable broth

- 1 can (13.5-ounce) full-fat coconut milk
- ½ cup frozen green peas
- Juice of ½ lime

Garnish

- Lime wedges
- Cilantro

Instructions:

1. Preheat your oven to 425 degrees F.
2. Spread the sweet potato noodles on a baking sheet in a single layer and bake for 10 minutes
3. Sauté onion with 3 tablespoons water in a soup pot for 6 minutes.
4. Stir in ginger, garlic, and red bell pepper, and cook for 2 minutes.
5. Add curry powder, broth, and milk, then cook for 15 minutes on medium-high heat.
6. Stir in lime juice and green peas.
7. Garnish with lime wedges and cilantro.
8. Serve warm.

Serving Suggestion:

Add some spiralized zucchini ribbons or mung bean sprouts on top of the soup before serving; they are great for the look and the taste.

Storage Tips:

Pour the leftover soup into a sealable container, cover the lid and freeze for no more than 3 months, or refrigerate for no more than 2 days.

Cream of Asparagus Soup

Nutritional Values Per Serving

Calories	364
Total Fat	29.9g
Saturated Fat	15.2g
Cholesterol	0mg
Sodium	1848mg
Total Carbohydrate	19g
Dietary Fiber	7.4g
Total Sugars	9.5g
Protein	11.4g

 Servings 4

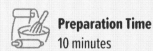 **Preparation Time** 10 minutes

 Cooking Time 22 minutes

Ingredients:

- 2 cups sweet onion, diced
- 4 tablespoon olive oil
- 2 garlic cloves, crushed
- 2 teaspoons salt
- ¼ teaspoon black pepper
- 2 lbs. asparagus, cut into 2-inch pieces
- 1 teaspoon rosemary fresh, chopped
- 1 teaspoon thyme fresh, chopped
- 3 ½ cups vegetable broth
- 1 (15-ounce) can coconut milk full-fat
- 1 ½ tablespoon lemon juice
- Parsley, to garnish

Instructions:

1. Add onion and 2 tablespoons oil to a Dutch oven and sauté for 5 minutes on medium heat.
2. Stir in crushed garlic, black pepper, and salt, then cook for 2 minutes.
3. Add remaining oil and asparagus, then cook for 5 minutes.
4. Stir in herbs, broth, and milk, then cover and cook for 10 minutes on a simmer.
5. Puree in a blender until smooth.
6. Stir in lemon juice and parsley.
7. Serve warm.

Serving Suggestion:

Add pieces of roasted asparagus on top of the soup before serving.

Storage Tips:

This soup is best stored in a freezer, and to do so, pack it in a small ziplock bag or reaction-free container.

The 30-Minute Gluten-free Vegan Cookbook for Beginners
150 simple, delicious, and nutritious whole food, plant-based, and Gluten-free recipes. Make them in under 30 minutes to improve your health and lose weight

63

Creamy Cauliflower Soup

Nutritional Values Per Serving	
Calories	255
Total Fat	15.6g
Saturated Fat	2.6 g
Cholesterol	0 mg
Sodium	1070 mg
Total Carbohydrate	24.3g
Dietary Fiber	7g
Total Sugars	7.3g
Protein	10.3g

 Servings 4

 Preparation Time 5 minutes

 Cooking Time 17 minutes

Ingredients:

- 1 cup onion, chopped
- ¼ cup carrot, chopped
- ½ cup celery, chopped
- 4 cloves garlic, minced
- 2 tablespoons almond butter
- 6 cups cauliflower, chopped

- 3 cups vegetable broth
- 1 tablespoon nutritional yeast flakes
- 1½ teaspoon salt
- 1½ teaspoon onion powder
- ½ teaspoon garlic powder
- ⅔ cup raw cashews

Instructions:

1. Sauté onion with celery, carrot, and garlic with almond butter in a soup pot for 7 minutes.

2. Stir in cauliflower, vegetable broth, seasonings, and yeast, then cook on a simmer for 10 minutes

3. Puree this soup with cashews and yeast in a blender until smooth.

4. Serve warm.

Serving Suggestion:

Add roasted cauliflower florets on top of the soup before serving.

Storage Tips:

Pack the soup in a food-grade ziplock bag, flatten this bag and freeze for up to 3 months. Let the soup freeze for 24 hours before stacking other soup packets on top.

CHAPTER 04

DELICIOUS, QUICK, AND EASY BREAKFAST MILLET

Porridge

Nutritional Values Per Serving

Calories	225
Total Fat	2.9g
Saturated Fat	0.1g
Cholesterol	0mg
Sodium	52mg
Total Carbohydrate	43.6g
Dietary Fiber	8.2g
Total Sugars	6.4g
Protein	6.2g

 Servings 4

 Preparation Time 5 minutes

 Cooking Time 25 minutes

Ingredients:

- 1 cup uncooked hulled millet
- 1 cup unsweetened almond milk
- 3 cups water
- 2 tablespoons maple syrup
- 1 tablespoon vanilla extract
- Sliced strawberries for topping
- Chopped almonds for topping

Instructions:

1. Mix millet with almond milk and water in a saucepan and cook to a boil.
2. Cover, reduce the heat, and cook for 20 minutes on medium-high heat.
3. Stir in vanilla, maple, fruit, and almonds.
4. Serve hot.

Serving Suggestion:

Serve this porridge with our gluten-free pumpkin bread.

Storage Tips:

Do not add the toppings if you wish to store the cooked porridge. Keep this porridge in a sealable mason jar and refrigerate for no more than 2 days. Add the toppings right before serving.

66

The 30-Minute Gluten-free Vegan Cookbook for Beginners
150 simple, delicious, and nutritious whole food, plant-based, and Gluten-free recipes. Make them in under 30 minutes to improve your health and lose weight

Creamy Crepes

Nutritional Values Per Serving	
Calories	343
Total Fat	20.2g
Saturated Fat	7.8g
Cholesterol	82mg
Sodium	202mg
Total Carbohydrate	31.4g
Dietary Fiber	3.6g
Total Sugars	15.2g
Protein	11.7g

 Servings
6

 Preparation Time
10 minutes

 Cooking Time
8 minutes

Ingredients:

- ¼ cup white rice flour
- ¼ cup sorghum flour
- ¼ cup almond flour
- 1 ¾ cups almond milk
- 6 tablespoons flaxseeds

- 12 tablespoons water
- ⅓ cup avocado oil
- 1 teaspoon vanilla extract
- ¼ teaspoon salt

Cashew Coconut Cream

- ½ cup cashews, soaked
- ½ cup coconut cream
- 1 teaspoon espresso powder
- ¼ cup maple syrup

- 2 tablespoons almond milk
- 1 tablespoon lemon juice
- Pinch of salt
- 1 banana

Instructions:

1. Soak flax seeds in water in a bowl for 5 minutes to make flaxseed eggs.

2. Blend cashews with coconut cream, espresso powder, maple syrup, almond milk, lemon juice, salt, and banana in a blender, and keep this filling aside.

3. Mix all the flours with flaxseed eggs, vanilla, salt, and almond milk in a bowl until smooth.

4. Set a skillet over medium heat and grease it with avocado oil.

5. Pour ¼ cup of the batter into the skillet, let it spread evenly, and cook for 2 minutes per side.

6. Make more pancakes in the same way.

7. Divide the prepared filling over the pancakes.

8. Roll the pancakes and serve.

Serving Suggestion:

If you are not a sweet cashew filling fan, then you can simply add sliced banana or tofu scramble to stuff these crepes.

Storage Tips:

Cooked crepes tend to get soggy over time, so you can store the uncooked batter and creamy filling in your refrigerator to cook and cook a batch any time you want.

The 30-Minute Gluten-free Vegan Cookbook for Beginners
150 simple, delicious, and nutritious whole food, plant-based, and Gluten-free recipes. Make them in under 30 minutes to improve your health and lose weight

67

Sweet Potato Pancakes

Nutritional Values Per Serving

Calories	272
Total Fat	14.8g
Saturated Fat	1.3g
Cholesterol	0mg
Sodium	183mg
Total Carbohydrate	28.8g
Dietary Fiber	5.2g
Total Sugars	12.8g
Protein	6.9g

 Servings 4

 Preparation Time 10 minutes

 Cooking Time 8 minutes

Ingredients:

- 1 cup sweet potato puree
- 2 tablespoons flaxseeds
- 4 tablespoons water
- 2 tablespoons melted almond butter
- ⅔ cup almond flour
- 2 teaspoons baking powder
- 3 tablespoons maple sugar
- ¼ teaspoon sea salt
- 1 teaspoon vanilla extract
- ⅔ teaspoon cinnamon
- ¼ teaspoon cardamom

Instructions:

1. Soak flax seeds in water in a bowl for 5 minutes to make a flaxseed egg.
2. Mix sweet potato puree with flaxseed egg and maple sugar in a bowl.
3. Stir in the rest of the recipe ingredients and mix well until lump-free.
4. Place a nonstick griddle over medium heat.
5. Pour ¼ cup of the batter over the griddle and cook for 2 minutes per side.
6. Make more sweet potato pancakes in the same way.
7. Serve.

Serving Suggestion:

Enjoy these pancakes with a berry smoothie.

Storage Tips:

Keep the uncooked pancake batter stored in a nozzle bottle in your refrigerator for no more than 2-3 days and pour it out to make pancakes every day.

Berry Smoothie

Nutritional Values Per Serving	
Calories	287
Total Fat	2.6g
Saturated Fat	0.3g
Cholesterol	0mg
Sodium	226mg
Total Carbohydrate	50.6g
Dietary Fiber	11.1g
Total Sugars	23g
Protein	18.4g

 Servings 2

 Preparation Time 5 minutes

 Cooking Time 0 minutes

Ingredients:

- 1 cup fresh strawberries
- 1 cup blueberries
- 1 banana, sliced
- ½ cup white beans, cooked and drained
- ½ cup soy milk
- 1 cup cauliflower, frozen
- 1 teaspoon vanilla extract
- 1 scoop of vegan protein powder

Toppings

- Hemp seeds
- Crushed almonds
- Fresh blueberries

Instructions:

1. Blend strawberries with blueberries, banana, white beans, soy milk, cauliflower, vanilla, and protein powder in a high-speed blender until smooth.
2. Garnish with hemp seeds, almonds, and blueberries.
3. Serve.

Serving Suggestion:

Serve this smoothie with some oat muffins.

Storage Tips:

You can refrigerate or freeze this smoothie in a sealable bottle.

The 30-Minute Gluten-free Vegan Cookbook for Beginners
150 simple, delicious, and nutritious whole food, plant-based, and Gluten-free recipes. Make them in under 30 minutes to improve your health and lose weight

69

Oat Pancakes

Nutritional Values Per Serving	
Calories	306
Total Fat	10.8g
Saturated Fat	2g
Cholesterol	3mg
Sodium	304mg
Total Carbohydrate	42g
Dietary Fiber	5.4g
Total Sugars	15.9g
Protein	9.7g

 Servings 6

 Preparation Time 10 minutes

 Cooking Time 12 minutes

Ingredients:

- 2 cups oat flour
- 3 tablespoon arrowroot flour
- ½ cup maple sugar
- 4 tablespoons flaxseeds
- 8 tablespoons water
- 1 cup vegan buttermilk

- 1⅓ cups coconut yogurt
- 4 tablespoon almond butter, melted
- 1 tablespoon vanilla extract
- 1½ teaspoon baking powder
- ¾ teaspoon baking soda

- ¼ teaspoon salt
- 1 teaspoon lemon juice

Vegan buttermilk

- 1 cup almond milk
- 1 tablespoon apple cider vinegar

Instructions:

1. Mix flaxseeds with water in a bowl and soak for 5 minutes.
2. Add almond milk and apple cider vinegar to a bowl to make the buttermilk and keep it aside.
3. Mix oat flour with arrowroot flour, salt, sweetener, baking powder, and baking soda in a bowl.
4. Stir in buttermilk, vanilla, almond butter, flaxseed eggs, and lemon juice.
5. Add coconut yogurt and mix well until the batter is lump-free.
6. Set a nonstick griddle over low, medium heat.
7. Pour ¼ cup of this batter over the griddle and cook for 2-3 minutes per side until golden brown.
8. Make more pancakes in the same way.
9. Serve.

Serving Suggestion:

Drizzle some maple syrup and dark chocolate syrup on top of the pancakes before serving.

Storage Tips:

Keep the uncooked pancake batter stored in a nozzle bottle in your refrigerator for no more than 2-3 days and pour it out to make pancakes every day.

Sweet Potato Smoothie

Nutritional Values Per Serving	
Calories	365
Total Fat	6.6g
Saturated Fat	0.8g
Cholesterol	0mg
Sodium	43mg
Total Carbohydrate	73.8g
Dietary Fiber	15.5g
Total Sugars	36g
Protein	8.2g

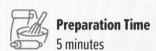 **Servings** 2

 **Preparation Time** 5 minutes

Cooking Time 0 minutes

Ingredients:

- 1 large sweet potato, roasted and cubed
- 2 medium bananas, sliced
- ½ cup rolled oats
- ¼ cup unsweetened soy milk
- 1 teaspoon vanilla extract
- ½ teaspoon cinnamon

Toppings

- ½ mango, peeled and diced
- 1 tablespoon chia seeds
- ½ cup fresh raspberries
- 1 small kiwi, sliced
- Fresh mint leaves, chopped

Instructions:

1. Blend sweet potato with bananas, oats, soy milk, vanilla, and cinnamon in a blender until smooth.
2. Garnish the smoothie with mango, chia seeds, raspberries, kiwi, and mint.
3. Serve.

Storage Tips:

Do not add toppings if you want to store the smoothie. You can refrigerate or freeze this smoothie in a sealable bottle.

The 30-Minute Gluten-free Vegan Cookbook for Beginners
150 simple, delicious, and nutritious whole food, plant-based, and Gluten-free recipes. Make them in under 30 minutes to improve your health and lose weight

71

Breakfast Casserole

  Servings
8

 **Preparation Time**
8 minutes

 Cooking Time
20 minutes

Nutritional Values Per Serving

Calories	317
Total Fat	5.5g
Saturated Fat	1.3g
Cholesterol	0mg
Sodium	97mg
Total Carbohydrate	54.6g
Dietary Fiber	13.7g
Total Sugars	8.9g
Protein	13.9g

Ingredients:

- 20 ounces potato hashbrowns, shredded
- 1 cup mushrooms, chopped
- 1 cup Vidalia onion, chopped
- 1 cup red bell pepper, chopped
- 1 cup tomatoes, chopped
- 1 cup spinach, chopped
- 1 teaspoon garlic, minced
- 2 cups vegan cheddar cheese, shredded
- Chopped scallions to garnish

Chickpea Egg

- 2 ½ cups chickpea flour
- 4 cups water
- 2 tablespoons nutritional yeast
- 1 teaspoon turmeric
- ½ teaspoon black pepper

Instructions:

1. Preheat the oven to 450 degrees F.
2. Mix chickpea flour with water, yeast, turmeric, and black pepper in a bowl.
3. Grease a 9x13-inch casserole dish with oil.
4. Spread the hashbrowns in the dish and top them with veggies and 1 cup cheese.
5. Pour the chickpea mixture into the casserole dish and add the remaining cheese and scallions on top.
6. Bake the breakfast casserole for 20 minutes until golden brown.
7. Serve hot.

Storage Tips:

Place the casserole in a sealable container and refrigerate for no more than 3 days or freeze for 3 months. Let it thaw first at room temperature before reheating.

The 30-Minute Gluten-free Vegan Cookbook for Beginners
150 simple, delicious, and nutritious whole food, plant-based, and Gluten-free recipes. Make them in under 30 minutes to improve your health and lose weight

Healthy Granola

 Servings
8

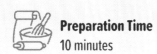 **Preparation Time**
10 minutes

 Cooking Time
20 minutes

Nutritional Values Per Serving	
Calories	269
Total Fat	12.7g
Saturated Fat	1.6g
Cholesterol	0mg
Sodium	77mg
Total Carbohydrate	36g
Dietary Fiber	3g
Total Sugars	16.5g
Protein	3.8g

Ingredients:

- ¼ cup olive oil
- ⅔ cup maple syrup
- 1 tablespoon vanilla extract
- 2 teaspoons cinnamon
- ½ teaspoon allspice
- ¼ teaspoon salt
- 3 cups old-fashioned oats
- 3 cups puffed rice
- 1 cup pecan halves

Instructions:

1. Preheat the oven to 400 degrees F.
2. Mix maple syrup, oil, vanilla, cinnamon, allspice, and salt in a large bowl.
3. Toss in oats, puffed rice, and pecans, then toss well to coat.
4. Spread this granola evenly on a baking sheet lined with parchment paper.
5. Bake the granola mixture for 20 minutes.
6. Serve.

Serving Suggestion:

Enjoy this granola with your favorite vegan smoothie.

Storage Tips:

Store the granola in a cookie jar or any glass jar at room temperature.

The 30-Minute Gluten-free Vegan Cookbook for Beginners
150 simple, delicious, and nutritious whole food, plant-based, and Gluten-free recipes. Make them in under 30 minutes to improve your health and lose weight

73

Banana Waffles

Nutritional Values Per Serving

Calories	144
Total Fat	8.6g
Saturated Fat	6g
Cholesterol	0mg
Sodium	177mg
Total Carbohydrate	16.2g
Dietary Fiber	1.2g
Total Sugars	2.3g
Protein	1.4g

 Servings 4

 Preparation Time 10 minutes

 Cooking Time 15 minutes

Ingredients:

- 1 ¼ cups unsweetened almond milk
- ¼ cup coconut oil, melted
- 2 teaspoons pure vanilla extract
- 2 tablespoons ground flax seed
- ½ cup puréed bananas
- 2 cups almond flour
- 1 tablespoon baking powder
- ½ teaspoon baking soda
- 1 teaspoon ground cinnamon
- ½ teaspoon ground nutmeg
- ¼ teaspoon salt

Instructions:

1. Preheat your waffle machine as per the machine's instructions.
2. Mix almond milk with coconut oil, vanilla, flaxseeds, and banana in a bowl.
3. Stir in baking soda, flour, baking powder, cinnamon, salt, and nutmeg, then mix well until smooth.
4. Leave this mixture to sit for 5 minutes.
5. Pour a dollop of this batter into the waffle iron and cook for 3-5 minutes until golden brown.
6. Make more waffles in the same way.
7. Serve.

Serving Suggestion:

Serve these waffles with maple syrup on top.

Storage Tips:

Instead of storing cooked waffles, store the uncooked batter in a container and refrigerate it for no more than 3 days.

Peanut Butter Breakfast Bars

Nutritional Values Per Serving	
Calories	255
Total Fat	11.6g
Saturated Fat	1.7g
Cholesterol	0mg
Sodium	193mg
Total Carbohydrate	31.8g
Dietary Fiber	5.7g
Total Sugars	12.3g
Protein	7.2g

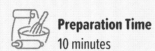 **Servings**
8

 Preparation Time
10 minutes

Cooking Time
20 minutes

Ingredients:

- 1 ½ cups quick-cooking oats
- ½ cup almond meal
- ½ cup flaxseed meal
- 2 teaspoon ground cinnamon
- ½ teaspoon sea salt
- 4 tablespoons vegan vanilla protein powder

- 1 teaspoon pure vanilla extract
- 2 bananas, ripe and mashed
- ½ cup applesauce
- ¼ cup creamy peanut butter
- 2 tablespoons maple syrup

Instructions:

1. Preheat oven to 400 degrees F.
2. Grease an 8x8-inch baking dish with cooking spray.
3. Toss oats with almond meal, flaxseed, salt, protein powder, and cinnamon in a bowl.
4. Stir in banana, applesauce, vanilla, maple syrup, and peanut butter.
5. Mix evenly, then spread this mixture in the baking dish.
6. Bake the casserole for 20 minutes until golden brown.
7. Cut the baked casserole into bars and serve.

Serving Suggestion:

Drizzle cinnamon and melted peanut butter on top before serving.

Storage Tips:

Keep the bars in a sealable container and refrigerate for no more than 2 days or freeze for 3 months. Make sure to reheat the bars in the oven to remove their moisture.

The 30-Minute Gluten-free Vegan Cookbook for Beginners
150 simple, delicious, and nutritious whole food, plant-based, and Gluten-free recipes. Make them in under 30 minutes to improve your health and lose weight

75

Cauliflower Oatmeal

 Servings 2

 Preparation Time 5 minutes

 Cooking Time 10 minutes

Nutritional Values Per Serving	
Calories	149
Total Fat	6.5g
Saturated Fat	1.9g
Cholesterol	0mg
Sodium	304mg
Total Carbohydrate	15.6g
Dietary Fiber	0.9g
Total Sugars	8.7g
Protein	9.1g

Ingredients:

- 1 cup cauliflower rice
- ½ cup unsweetened almond milk
- ½ teaspoon cinnamon
- ¼ teaspoon stevia
- ½ tablespoon peanut butter
- 1 strawberry, sliced

Instructions:

1. Add cauliflower rice, almond milk, stevia, and cinnamon to a saucepan and cook for 10 minutes on a simmer.
2. Stir in the rest of the ingredients and serve.

Serving Suggestion:

Add blueberries, raspberries, and apple slices to the oatmeal for an enhanced taste.

Storage Tips:

Divide the oatmeal into 2 mason jars and refrigerate for no more than 2 days for storage.

Chocolate Pancakes

 **Servings** 6

 **Preparation Time** 10 minutes

Cooking Time 15 minutes

Nutritional Values Per Serving	
Calories	231
Total Fat	9.1g
Saturated Fat	6.6g
Cholesterol	2mg
Sodium	352mg
Total Carbohydrate	36.8g
Dietary Fiber	4.8g
Total Sugars	17.2g
Protein	4.8g

Ingredients:

- 1 ¼ cups oat flour
- ½ cup cocoa powder
- 1 ¼ teaspoons baking soda
- ¼ teaspoon sea salt
- ½ cup apple sauce
- ½ cup unsweetened almond milk
- 6 tablespoons maple syrup
- 1 tablespoon apple cider vinegar
- ¼ cup chocolate chips

Instructions:

1. Mix oat flour with cocoa powder, baking soda, salt, apple sauce, milk, maple syrup, and apple cider vinegar in a bowl.
2. Fold in chocolate chips and mix evenly.
3. Set a griddle pan over medium heat.
4. Pour ¼ cup of batter on the griddle and cook for 2-3 minutes per side until golden brown.
5. Make more pancakes in the same way.
6. Serve.

Serving Suggestion:

Top these pancakes with some chocolate chips and maple syrup before serving.

Storage Tips:

Keep the uncooked pancake batter stored in a nozzle bottle in your refrigerator for no more than 2-3 days and pour it out to make pancakes every day.

The 30-Minute Gluten-free Vegan Cookbook for Beginners
150 simple, delicious, and nutritious whole food, plant-based, and Gluten-free recipes. Make them in under 30 minutes to improve your health and lose weight

77

Chocolate Chia Pudding

Nutritional Values Per Serving

Calories	210
Total Fat	16g
Saturated Fat	7.4g
Cholesterol	0mg
Sodium	10mg
Total Carbohydrate	14.3g
Dietary Fiber	10.8g
Total Sugars	1g
Protein	5.6g

 Servings 4

 Preparation Time 25 minutes

 Cooking Time 0 minutes

Ingredients:

- ½ cup almond milk
- ½ cup water
- 1 tablespoon cocoa powder
- 4 tablespoons chia seeds
- 6 drops Lakanto Liquid Monkfruit Sweetener
- 1 teaspoon maca powder

Instructions:

1. Mix chia seeds with cocoa powder and the rest of the ingredients in a mason jar.
2. Cover this jar and refrigerate for 20 minutes.
3. Serve.

Serving Suggestion:

Add mixed berries and chopped nuts on top of the pudding.

Storage Tips:

Divide the pudding into four small mason jars, seal the lid and refrigerate for no more than 3 days.

Tofu Oatmeal Muffins

Nutritional Values Per Serving

Calories	198
Total Fat	3.1g
Saturated Fat	0.5g
Cholesterol	0mg
Sodium	294mg
Total Carbohydrate	34.3g
Dietary Fiber	6g
Total Sugars	4.1g
Protein	7.1g

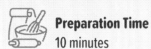 **Servings** 4

 Preparation Time 10 minutes

Cooking Time 20 minutes

Ingredients:

- 2 cups quick oats
- 1 ½ teaspoons baking powder
- 2 teaspoons cinnamon
- ½ teaspoon salt
- 1 cup granulated Lakanto Monk fruit Sweetener
- 1 package (14-ounce) organic tofu, firm
- 1 teaspoon vanilla extract
- ½ teaspoon liquid stevia extract
- ½ cup applesauce
- ½ cup water

Instructions:

1. Preheat the oven to 400 degrees F.
2. Line a muffin tray with a cupcake liner.
3. Blend oats with the rest of the muffin ingredients in a blender.
4. Divide this oat batter into the muffin cups and bake for 20 minutes until golden brown.
5. Serve.

Storage Tips:

Keep the muffins in a sealable container and refrigerate for no more than 2 days or freeze for 3 months. Make sure to reheat the muffins in the oven to remove their moisture.

The 30-Minute Gluten-free Vegan Cookbook for Beginners
150 simple, delicious, and nutritious whole food, plant-based, and Gluten-free recipes. Make them in under 30 minutes to improve your health and lose weight

79

Millet Butter Waffles

Nutritional Values Per Serving	
Calories	197
Total Fat	9.2g
Saturated Fat	0.5g
Cholesterol	0mg
Sodium	73mg
Total Carbohydrate	27.1g
Dietary Fiber	4.3g
Total Sugars	8.3g
Protein	6g

 Servings 4

 Preparation Time 10 minutes

 Cooking Time 15 minutes

Ingredients:

- ½ cup unsweetened vanilla almond milk
- 1 small ripe peeled banana
- 4 tablespoons creamy almond butter
- 1 tablespoon maple syrup
- ⅛ teaspoon salt
- ½ cup millet flour

Instructions:

1. Mix almond milk, banana, almond butter, maple syrup, salt, and millet flour in a bowl until lump-free.
2. Heat your waffle iron and add a dollop of batter to it.
3. Cook this waffle for 5 minutes until golden brown.
4. Make more waffles in the same way.
5. Serve.

Serving Suggestion:

Top the waffles with maple syrup and then add some banana slices over them.

Storage Tips:

Instead of storing cooked waffles, store the uncooked batter in a container and refrigerate it for no more than 3 days.

Vegan Oat Muffins

Nutritional Values Per Serving	
Calories	165
Total Fat	9.9g
Saturated Fat	1.5g
Cholesterol	0mg
Sodium	95mg
Total Carbohydrate	15.3g
Dietary Fiber	12g
Total Sugars	0.2g
Protein	7.5g

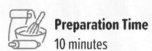

Servings
4

Preparation Time
10 minutes

Cooking Time
25 minutes

Ingredients:

- 2 tablespoons flaxseeds
- ¼ cup and 6 tablespoons of water
- ½ cup ground flaxseeds
- ¼ cup oat fiber
- ½ cup granulated Lakanto Monk Fruit Sweetener

- 2 tablespoons coconut flour
- 1 teaspoon cinnamon
- ½ teaspoon baking powder
- ¼ teaspoon baking soda
- ¼ teaspoon vanilla extract

Instructions:

1. Preheat the oven to 400 degrees F.
2. Grease a muffin pan with cooking spray.
3. Mix flaxseeds with 6 tablespoons of water in a mixing bowl and leave it for 5 minutes.
4. Stir in the oats and the rest of the ingredients, then mix well.
5. Divide this oats mixture into the muffin cups and bake for 25 minutes.
6. Serve.

Serving Suggestion:

Add chopped nuts on top of the freshly baked muffins.

Storage Tips:

Keep the muffins in a sealable container and refrigerate for no more than 2 days or freeze for 3 months. Make sure to reheat the muffins in the oven to remove their moisture.

The 30-Minute Gluten-free Vegan Cookbook for Beginners
150 simple, delicious, and nutritious whole food, plant-based, and Gluten-free recipes. Make them in under 30 minutes to improve your health and lose weight

81

Gluten-free Pumpkin Bread

Nutritional Values Per Serving

Calories	276
Total Fat	10.4g
Saturated Fat	1g
Cholesterol	0mg
Sodium	100mg
Total Carbohydrate	38.2g
Dietary Fiber	3.7g
Total Sugars	17.3g
Protein	6.8g

 Servings 6

 Preparation Time 10 minutes

 Cooking Time 25 minutes

Ingredients:

- ¼ cup coconut oil
- ⅔ cup unsweetened almond milk
- 1 cup pumpkin purée
- 1 tablespoon apple cider vinegar
- 8 tablespoons maple syrup
- 1 teaspoon vanilla extract
- Pinch or salt

- 1¼ cups ground almonds
- 1¼ cups almond flour
- 4 teaspoons baking powder
- ¼ teaspoon bicarbonate of soda
- 2 teaspoons pumpkin pie spice
- ½ teaspoon ground ginger

Instructions:

1. Preheat the oven to 450 degrees F.
2. Mix almond milk with coconut oil, pumpkin puree, apple cider vinegar, maple syrup, vanilla, salt, and ground almonds in a bowl.
3. Stir in flour, baking powder, bicarbonate of soda, pumpkin pie spice, and ginger.
4. Mix well and divide the batter into ½-pound loaf pans.
5. Place the pans in a roasting pan and bake for 25 minutes until golden brown.
6. Serve.

Serving Suggestion:

Sprinkle roasted pumpkin seeds over the bread before the last 5 minutes of baking for a crunchy crust.

Storage Tips:

Keep the bread wrapped in a plastic bag, seal this bag to avoid moisture, and refrigerate for no more than 4-5 days.

The 30-Minute Gluten-free Vegan Cookbook for Beginners
150 simple, delicious, and nutritious whole food, plant-based, and Gluten-free recipes. Make them in under 30 minutes to improve your health and lose weight

Blueberry Baked Oatmeal

Nutritional Values Per Serving	
Calories	113
Total Fat	2.3g
Saturated Fat	0.2g
Cholesterol	0mg
Sodium	73mg
Total Carbohydrate	21.6g
Dietary Fiber	2.5g
Total Sugars	9.3g
Protein	2.5g

 Servings
4

 **Preparation Time**
10 minutes

 **Cooking Time**
20 minutes

Ingredients:

- 1 banana, peeled
- 1 cup rolled oats
- ⁴⁄₅ cup unsweetened almond milk
- 1 cup blueberries
- ½ teaspoon ground cinnamon

Instructions:

1. Preheat the oven to 400 degrees F.
2. Mash banana in a bowl, then stir in almond milk, oats, blueberries, and cinnamon.
3. Mix well and spread this batter into a greased baking pan.
4. Bake this oatmeal for 20 minutes until golden brown.
5. Serve.

Storage Tips:

Place the baked oatmeal in a sealable container and refrigerate for no more than 3 days for storage.

The 30-Minute Gluten-free Vegan Cookbook for Beginners
150 simple, delicious, and nutritious whole food, plant-based, and Gluten-free recipes. Make them in under 30 minutes to improve your health and lose weight

83

Pumpkin Pancakes

Nutritional Values Per Serving

Calories	392
Total Fat	12.3g
Saturated Fat	6g
Cholesterol	0mg
Sodium	240mg
Total Carbohydrate	68.1g
Dietary Fiber	2.2g
Total Sugars	5.8g
Protein	4.8g

 Servings 6

 Preparation Time 10 minutes

 Cooking Time 15 minutes

Ingredients:

- 1 ½ cups unsweetened almond milk
- ½ cup unsweetened pumpkin puree
- 3 tablespoons coconut oil
- 1 teaspoon pure vanilla extract
- 2 tablespoons ground flax seeds
- 2 tablespoons pure maple syrup
- 2 cups almond flour
- 1 tablespoon baking powder
- ½ teaspoon baking soda
- 2 teaspoons pumpkin pie spice
- ¼ teaspoon salt

Instructions:

1. Place almond milk, pumpkin puree, vanilla, oil, ground flaxseeds, and maple syrup in a bowl and leave for 5 minutes.
2. Stir in flour, baking powder, pumpkin pie spice, salt, and baking soda, then mix well until smooth.
3. Set a pan over medium-high heat.
4. Pour about 1/3 cup of the batter into the pan and cook for 2-3 minutes per side.
5. Make more pancakes in the same way.
6. Serve.

Serving Suggestion:

Drizzle maple syrup over the pancakes and then top them with chopped nuts, seeds, and blueberries.

Storage Tips:

Keep the uncooked pancake batter stored in a nozzle bottle in your refrigerator for no more than 2-3 days and pour it out to make pancakes every day.

Apple Steel Cut Oats

Nutritional Values Per Serving	
Calories	353
Total Fat	3.3g
Saturated Fat	0.6g
Cholesterol	0mg
Sodium	310mg
Total Carbohydrate	79.9g
Dietary Fiber	9.6g
Total Sugars	39.8g
Protein	7g

 Servings
2

 **Preparation Time**
10 minutes

 **Cooking Time**
10 minutes

Ingredients:

- 1 cup steel-cut oats
- ½ cup unsweetened plain applesauce
- 1 teaspoon ground cinnamon
- ½ teaspoon ground nutmeg
- ¼ teaspoon salt
- 3 cups water
- 1 small apple, chopped
- ½ cup raisins
- ¼ cup chopped nuts
- Sweetener, to taste

Instructions:

1. Add oats, applesauce, cinnamon, nutmeg, salt, and water to an Instant Pot.
2. Cover and seal the pressure lid and cook for 10 minutes on high pressure.
3. Once done, release the pressure completely and remove the lid.
4. Add apples, chopped nuts, sweetener, and raisins, then serve.

Serving Suggestion:

Top the oats with healthy granola before serving.

Storage Tips:

Keep the oatmeal in a mason jar and seal it to refrigerate for no more than 3 days.

The 30-Minute Gluten-free Vegan Cookbook for Beginners
150 simple, delicious, and nutritious whole food, plant-based, and Gluten-free recipes. Make them in under 30 minutes to improve your health and lose weight

85

CHAPTER 05

DELICIOUS, QUICK, AND EASY LUNCH RECIPES

Roasted Cauliflower and Chickpeas

Nutritional Values Per Serving	
Calories	333
Total Fat	3.8g
Saturated Fat	0.5g
Cholesterol	0mg
Sodium	51mg
Total Carbohydrate	64.4g
Dietary Fiber	10.7g
Total Sugars	9.7g
Protein	12.8g

 Servings 6

 Preparation Time 10 minutes

Cooking Time 20 minutes

Ingredients:

- ¼ cup and 2 tablespoons lemon juice
- 2 tablespoons pure maple syrup
- 4 garlic cloves, minced
- 1½ teaspoons paprika
- 1 teaspoon ground cumin
- ½ teaspoon ground cinnamon
- ½ teaspoon ground turmeric

- ¼ teaspoon ground coriander
- Sea salt, to taste
- Black pepper, to taste
- 2-lbs. head cauliflower, cut into florets (6 cups)
- 1 (15-ounce) can of chickpeas, rinsed, drained
- ¼ cup tahini

- ⅛ teaspoon cayenne pepper
- 2 cups cooked brown rice
- 1 medium cucumber, sliced
- 2 medium bell peppers, julienned
- ½ cup red onion, slivered
- Fresh cilantro leaves to garnish
- Lemon wedges to garnish

Instructions:

1. Preheat the oven to 500 degrees F.
2. Line a baking sheet with parchment paper.
3. Mix ¼ cup lemon juice, maple syrup, garlic, paprika, cumin, cinnamon, turmeric, coriander, salt, and black pepper in a large bowl.
4. Toss in chickpeas and cauliflower, then mix well.
5. Spread this chickpea mixture on the baking sheet and roast for 20 minutes.
6. Meanwhile, mix tahini with the remaining lemon juice, cayenne pepper, and 4 tablespoons of water in a bowl.
7. Add the cauliflower mixture, rice, cucumber, bell pepper, and red onion to a serving bowl.
8. Garnish with tahini mixture, cilantro leaves, and lemon wedges.
9. Serve warm.

Serving Suggestion:

Stuff this cauliflower and chickpea mix in gluten-free tortillas for serving.

Storage Tips:

This cauliflower and chickpea medley can be best stored in a refrigerator for no more than 3 days or in a freezer for up to 3 months, and to do so, pack it in a small ziplock bag or reaction-free container.

The 30-Minute Gluten-free Vegan Cookbook for Beginners
150 simple, delicious, and nutritious whole food, plant-based, and Gluten-free recipes. Make them in under 30 minutes to improve your health and lose weight

87

Meatless Stew

 Servings
4

 Preparation Time
10 minutes

 Cooking Time
25 minutes

Nutritional Values Per Serving	
Calories	318
Total Fat	2g
Saturated Fat	0.3g
Cholesterol	2mg
Sodium	87mg
Total Carbohydrate	68.7g
Dietary Fiber	14.3g
Total Sugars	16.3g
Protein	10.2g

Ingredients:

- 1½ large yellow onions, chopped
- 3 medium carrots, sliced
- 3 ribs celery, chopped
- 2 medium portobello mushrooms, chopped
- 6 garlic cloves, minced
- 2 lb. white potatoes, peeled and diced
- ⅓ cup tomato paste
- 1 tablespoon dried Italian seasoning
- 1 tablespoon paprika
- 2 teaspoons fresh rosemary, chopped
- 1½ cups thawed frozen peas
- ½ cup fresh parsley, chopped

Instructions:

1. Sauté onions with carrots, celery, and 1 tablespoon of water in a Dutch oven for 5 minutes.
2. Stir in mushrooms and garlic, then cook for 5 minutes.
3. Add potatoes, Italian seasoning, tomato paste, paprika, rosemary, and 5 cups of water.
4. Cook for almost 10 minutes on high heat, then add peas and cook for 5 minutes.
5. Puree the soup in a blender, then garnish with parsley.
6. Serve warm.

Serving Suggestion:

Enjoy this stew with white rice.

Storage Tips:

This meatless stew can be best stored in a freezer for no more than 3 months, and to do so, pack it in a small ziplock bag or reaction-free container.

Curried Millet Sushi

Nutritional Values Per Serving	
Calories	302
Total Fat	2.7g
Saturated Fat	0.5g
Cholesterol	0mg
Sodium	144mg
Total Carbohydrate	58g
Dietary Fiber	8.1g
Total Sugars	11.2g
Protein	8.6g

 Servings
4

 Preparation Time
10 minutes

 Cooking Time
10 minutes

Ingredients:

- 1 cup millet
- 1½ teaspoons curry powder
- 1½ teaspoons onion powder
- 1½ teaspoons garlic powder
- ¼ cup brown rice vinegar

- 2 tablespoons pure maple syrup
- 1½ teaspoons arrowroot powder
- ¼ teaspoon sea salt
- 4 toasted nori sheets

- 1 red bell pepper, cut into strips
- 1 cup carrots, shredded
- 2 small avocados, sliced
- 1 cup fresh spinach

Instructions:

1. Add millet, curry powder, onion powder, garlic powder, and 2 cups of water to an Instant Pot.
2. Seal the pressure cooker lid and cook on high pressure for 10 minutes
3. Once done, release the pressure completely, then remove the lid.
4. Mix brown rice vinegar, maple syrup, salt, and arrowroot powder in a bowl.
5. Add this mixture to the millet and mix well.
6. Place a nori sheet on the bamboo sheet and add ⅔ cup of the millet mixture on top.
7. Press the millet into an even layer to cover the nori sheet and leave ¼ inch spaces around the edges.
8. Then add ¼ of the vegetables, avocado, and spinach at the center of the millet layer.
9. Roll the nori sheet into a tight sushi roll and make more rolls in the same way.
10. Cut the sushi rolls into slices and serve.

Serving Suggestion:

Serve the sushi with tamari sauce and wasabi paste on the side.

Storage Tips:

Carefully place the sushi over a saran wrap sheet and wrap this sheet around to keep the sushi in place. Place the wrapped sushi in a sealable container and refrigerate for no more than 2 days.

The 30-Minute Gluten-free Vegan Cookbook for Beginners
150 simple, delicious, and nutritious whole food, plant-based, and Gluten-free recipes. Make them in under 30 minutes to improve your health and lose weight

89

Tofu Fried Rice

 Servings
4

 Preparation Time
10 minutes

Cooking Time
19 minutes

Nutritional Values Per Serving	
Calories	354
Total Fat	8g
Saturated Fat	1.7g
Cholesterol	0mg
Sodium	7778mq
Total Carbohydrate	61.2g
Dietary Fiber	1.5g
Total Sugars	35.2g
Protein	14g

Ingredients:

- 4 cups cooked long-grain rice, cooled
- 1 onion, chopped
- 4 garlic cloves, minced
- 8 ounces tofu, cut into small cubes
- 1 head of broccoli, chopped
- 2 tablespoons olive oil

Sauce

- 5 tablespoons tamari
- 2 tablespoons mirin
- 1 tablespoon miso paste
- ½ teaspoon toasted sesame oil
- 1 teaspoon sriracha

Garnish

- 3 spring onions, sliced
- Sesame seeds, to garnish

Instructions:

1. Mix tamari with mirin, miso paste, sesame oil, and sriracha in a bowl.
2. Sauté tofu with oil in a skillet until golden brown.
3. Stir in 1 tbsp sauce and cook for 1 minute, then transfer the tofu to a plate.
4. Add chopped onion and minced garlic to the same skillet and cook for 5 minutes.
5. Toss in broccoli and cook for 5 minutes.
6. Stir in cooked rice, remaining sauce, and tofu, then mix gently.
7. Cook for 2 minutes, then garnish and serve.

Serving Suggestion:

Enjoy the rice with a bowl of tofu curry on the side.

Storage Tips:

Transfer the rice to a sealable container or a food-grade ziplock bag, seal it, and refrigerate it for no more than 2 days or freeze it for up to 3 months.

Curried Tomato-Lentil Stew

Nutritional Values Per Serving	
Calories	246
Total Fat	1.5g
Saturated Fat	0.3g
Cholesterol	0mg
Sodium	52mg
Total Carbohydrate	41.1g
Dietary Fiber	13.6g
Total Sugars	12.7 g
Protein	13.4g

 Servings
4

 Preparation Time
10 minutes

Cooking Time
15 minutes

Ingredients:

- 1 cup brown lentils, rinsed and drained
- 1 cup onion, chopped
- 3 garlic cloves, minced
- 1 teaspoon grated fresh ginger
- 1 (14.5-ounces) can diced tomatoes, undrained
- 1 cup carrots, chopped
- 1 teaspoon curry powder
- 1 ½ cup water
- Sea salt and black pepper, to taste
- Snipped fresh cilantro to garnish

Instructions:

1. Sauté ginger, garlic, and onion in an Instant Pot for 5 minutes on Sauté mode.
2. Stir in curry powder, carrots, tomatoes, lentils, and water.
3. Cover the pressure lid, seal the pot and cook for 10 minutes on high pressure.
4. Garnish with cilantro and serve warm.

Serving Suggestion:

Serve this stew with a bowl of white rice on the side.

Storage Tips:

Transfer the soup to a food-grade plastic bag, flatten this bag and refrigerate for no more than 2 days or you can freeze it for up to 3 months.

The 30-Minute Gluten-free Vegan Cookbook for Beginners
150 simple, delicious, and nutritious whole food, plant-based, and Gluten-free recipes. Make them in under 30 minutes to improve your health and lose weight

91

Chickpea Curry

Nutritional Values Per Serving

Calories	457
Total Fat	13.1g
Saturated Fat	1.5g
Cholesterol	0mg
Sodium	54mg
Total Carbohydrate	67.5g
Dietary Fiber	18.8g
Total Sugars	12.5g
Protein	21.1g

 Servings 4

 Preparation Time 10 minutes

 Cooking Time 12 minutes

Ingredients:

Paste

- 2 tablespoon olive oil
- 1 onion, diced
- 1 teaspoon fresh or dried chili
- 9 garlic cloves, chopped
- 1 thumb-sized piece of ginger, peeled
- 1 tablespoon ground coriander
- 2 tablespoons ground cumin
- 1 tablespoon garam masala
- 2 tablespoon tomato purée

Curry

- 2 (14 ounces) cans chickpeas, drained
- 1 (14 ounces) can of chopped tomatoes
- 3 ½ ounces creamed coconut
- ½ small pack of coriander, chopped
- 1 ½ cup water
- 3 ½ ounces spinach

Instructions:

1. Sauté onion with 2 tablespoons oil and chili in a skillet for 5 minutes on high heat.
2. Blend sautéed onions with garlic, ginger, coriander, cumin, garam masala, tomato puree, and salt in a blender to make a paste.
3. Sauté this paste in a cooking pot for 2 minutes.
4. Add tomatoes, chickpeas, creamed coconut, water, and spinach, and cook for 5 minutes.
5. Garnish with coriander and serve warm.

Serving Suggestion:

Enjoy this curry with vegan fried rice.

Storage Tips:

Keep the chickpea curry in a sealable container and refrigerate for no more than 2 days or freeze it for up to 3 months.

Vegan Pulled Jackfruit

Nutritional Values Per Serving	
Calories	160
Total Fat	4g
Saturated Fat	0.8g
Cholesterol	0mg
Sodium	255mg
Total Carbohydrate	30.9g
Dietary Fiber	2.8g
Total Sugars	5.4g
Protein	2.3g

 Servings
4

 Preparation Time
10 minutes

Cooking Time
22 minutes

Ingredients:

- 1 tablespoon vegetable oil
- 1 red onion, chopped
- 1 teaspoon ground cinnamon
- 1 teaspoon cumin seeds
- 2 teaspoons smoked paprika
- 2 teaspoons hot chipotle sauce

- 1 tablespoon apple cider vinegar
- 4 tablespoons gluten-free vegan BBQ sauce
- 1 (7-ounce) can of chopped tomato
- 2 (14-ounce) cans of young jackfruit
- 1 cup water

Instructions:

1. Sauté onion with oil in an Instant Pot for 5 minutes on Sauté mode.
2. Stir in cinnamon, paprika, and cumin, then cook for 2 minutes.
3. Stir in hot sauce, bbq sauce, apple cider vinegar, tomato, jackfruit, and water.
4. Cover the pressure lid, seal the pot and cook for 15 minutes.
5. Once done, release the pressure completely, then remove the lid.
6. Shred the jackfruit with a fork and mix well with its sauce.
7. Serve.

Serving Suggestion:

Stuff the jackfruit into gluten-free bread before serving.

Storage Tips:

Pack the pulled jackfruit in a small ziplock bag or reaction-free container and refrigerate for no more than 3 days or you can freeze it for 3 months.

The 30-Minute Gluten-free Vegan Cookbook for Beginners
150 simple, delicious, and nutritious whole food, plant-based, and Gluten-free recipes. Make them in under 30 minutes to improve your health and lose weight

93

Miso Glazed Mushrooms

Nutritional Values Per Serving	
Calories	178
Total Fat	1.1g
Saturated Fat	0.1g
Cholesterol	0mg
Sodium	2911mg
Total Carbohydrate	33.4g
Dietary Fiber	3.9g
Total Sugars	18.9g
Protein	12.6g

 Servings 2

 Preparation Time 10 minutes

Cooking Time 16 minutes

Ingredients:

- 14 ounces button mushrooms
- 1 medium onion, chopped
- ⅓ cup tamari
- 2 teaspoons gluten-free miso paste
- 2 tablespoons apple cider vinegar
- 2 tablespoons maple syrup
- 2 tablespoons water
- 1 teaspoon arrowroot powder

Instructions:

1. Boil mushrooms in a pot filled with water for 10 minutes, then drain.
2. Sauté onion in a frying pan for 3 minutes.
3. Mix tamari, apple cider vinegar, miso paste, arrowroot powder, maple, and water in a bowl.
4. Add mushrooms to the pan and pour in the glaze.
5. Cook for 3 minutes while mixing it well.
6. Serve warm.

Serving Suggestion:

Serve the mushrooms on top of sauteed zucchini noodles.

Storage Tips:

Keep the mushrooms in a sealable glass container and refrigerate for no more than 3 days. Reheat in the microwave before serving.

Tofu Curry

Nutritional Values Per Serving	
Calories	283
Total Fat	13.8g
Saturated Fat	4.7g
Cholesterol	0mg
Sodium	26mg
Total Carbohydrate	26.1g
Dietary Fiber	5.2g
Total Sugars	2.3g
Protein	14.5g

 Servings
4

 Preparation Time
10 minutes

 Cooking Time
20 minutes

Ingredients:

Curry

- 2 tablespoons almond butter
- 1 onion, chopped
- 2 teaspoons garam masala
- 2 teaspoons ground coriander
- 2 teaspoons ground cumin
- 2 teaspoons ground turmeric
- 1 garlic clove, chopped
- 1 thumb-size piece of fresh ginger, chopped
- 1 tablespoon tomato purée
- 2 cups canned tomatoes
- ¾ cup coconut cream
- Salt and black pepper to taste

Tofu puffs

- 2 (8 ounces) blocks of firm tofu
- 4 tablespoons corn flour
- 1 large pinch of salt
- Vegetable oil for frying

Instructions:

1. Grease a frying pan with almond butter.
2. Add 1 chopped onion with a pinch of salt, then sauté for 4 minutes.
3. Stir in spices, garlic, and ginger, then cook for 1 minute.
4. Then add tomato puree and cook for 2 minutes.
5. Stir in canned tomatoes and coconut cream then cook for 5 minutes on a boil with occasional stirring then reduce the heat to the lowest setting.
6. Meanwhile, cut the tofu into chunks.
7. Mix salt and corn flour in a bowl and coat the tofu chunks with this corn flour mixture.
8. Heat the vegetable oil in a suitable deep frying pan.
9. Shake off the excess corn flour and deep fry tofu for 5 minutes until golden brown.
10. Transfer the tofu to a plate using a slotted spoon.
11. Add the fried tofu to the curry.
12. Serve warm.

Serving Suggestion:

Serve this curry over a bowl of boiled rice.

Storage Tips:

Keep this tofu curry in a sealable storage container and refrigerate for no more than 2 days, or you can freeze it for up to 3 months. Reheat it at medium-low temperature before serving.

The 30-Minute Gluten-free Vegan Cookbook for Beginners
150 simple, delicious, and nutritious whole food, plant-based, and Gluten-free recipes. Make them in under 30 minutes to improve your health and lose weight

95

Vegetable Korma

Nutritional Values Per Serving	
Calories	304
Total Fat	7.1g
Saturated Fat	1g
Cholesterol	0mg
Sodium	56mg
Total Carbohydrate	57.7g
Dietary Fiber	7.4g
Total Sugars	18.8g
Protein	6.9g

 Servings 6

 Preparation Time 10 minutes

 Cooking Time 24 minutes

Ingredients:

- 2 tablespoon olive oil
- 1 onion, diced
- 2 garlic cloves, minced
- 2 tablespoon tomato paste
- 2 teaspoon garam masala
- 1 teaspoon curry powder
- 1 teaspoon turmeric
- ½ teaspoon coriander
- ½ teaspoon salt
- 1 can of coconut milk
- ½ cup vegetable broth
- 1 carrot, sliced
- 1 crown broccoli, cut into florets
- 1 large potato, cut into ½" cubes
- 1 cup frozen peas
- ¼ cup almonds, sliced

Instructions:

1. Sauté onion and garlic with olive oil in a sauté pan for 4 minutes.
2. Stir in tomato paste, curry powder, garam masala, turmeric, coriander, and salt.
3. Add broth and coconut milk, then cook to a simmer.
4. Stir in carrot, potato, broccoli, and peas, then cook for 20 minutes.
5. Garnish with sliced almonds and serve warm.

Serving Suggestion:

Enjoy this korma with boiled rice or with a gluten-free flatbread.

Storage Tips:

This vegetable korma can be best stored in a refrigerator for no more than 2 days or in a freezer for up to 3 months. To do so, pack it in a small ziplock bag or reaction-free container.

CHAPTER 06

DELICIOUS, QUICK, AND EASY DINNER RECIPES

Red Beans and Cauliflower Rice

Nutritional Values Per Serving

Calories	394
Total Fat	4.9g
Saturated Fat	1.1g
Cholesterol	1mg
Sodium	144mq
Total Carbohydrate	65.5g
Dietary Fiber	14.8g
Total Sugars	6.8g
Protein	25.1g

 Servings
6

 Preparation Time
10 minutes

 Cooking Time
17 minutes

Ingredients:

- 2 teaspoons olive oil
- ⅓ cup white onion, chopped
- ½ cup celery, chopped
- ½ cup green pepper, chopped
- 3 cups cauliflower rice
- 3 (15 ounces) cans of red beans, drained
- ½ teaspoon salt
- 2 teaspoons ground cumin
- 1 teaspoon paprika
- 1 teaspoon granulated garlic
- 1 teaspoon chili powder
- 1 teaspoon Italian seasoning
- ¼ teaspoon black pepper

Instructions:

1. Sauté the white onion with olive oil in a large pan for 2 minutes.
2. Toss in celery and green pepper, then cook for 5 minutes.
3. Add cauliflower rice, seasoning, spices, and beans then cook for 10 minutes.
4. Serve.

Serving Suggestion:

Serve the rice with some cucumber salad.

Storage Tips:

This red beans and cauliflower rice meal can be best stored in a refrigerator for no more than 3 days or in a freezer for up to 3 months, and to do so, pack it in a small ziplock bag or reaction-free container.

The 30-Minute Gluten-free Vegan Cookbook for Beginners
150 simple, delicious, and nutritious whole food, plant-based, and Gluten-free recipes. Make them in under 30 minutes to improve your health and lose weight

Quinoa Sweet Potatoes Curry

Nutritional Values Per Serving	
Calories	435
Total Fat	19.9g
Saturated Fat	15.4g
Cholesterol	0mg
Sodium	1088mg
Total Carbohydrate	54.6g
Dietary Fiber	8.9g
Total Sugars	12g
Protein	12.7g

 Servings
6

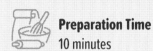 **Preparation Time**
10 minutes

 Cooking Time
30 minutes

Ingredients:

- 4 cups sweet potato, diced
- 1 cup quinoa, rinsed
- 1 cup brown lentils
- ½ yellow onion, diced
- 1 (15 ounces) can of coconut milk
- 3 ½ cups vegetable broth

- 2 teaspoons curry powder
- 1 ½ teaspoons salt
- 1 teaspoon ground ginger
- 1 teaspoon ground coriander
- 1 teaspoon granulated garlic
- ½ teaspoon black pepper

Garnish

- Chopped cashews
- Fresh cilantro, chopped

Instructions:

1. Add quinoa, sweet potato and the rest of the ingredients to a large cooking pot.
2. Cook this mixture to a boil on high heat, then reduce the heat to a medium-high.
3. Continue cooking this mixture for 25 minutes until the liquid is absorbed.
4. Garnish with cashews and cilantro.
5. Serve.

Serving Suggestion:

Enjoy this curry with some white rice.

Storage Tips:

This sweet potato curry can be best stored in a freezer for no more than 3 months, and to do so, pack it in a small ziplock bag or reaction-free container.

The 30-Minute Gluten-free Vegan Cookbook for Beginners
150 simple, delicious, and nutritious whole food, plant-based, and Gluten-free recipes. Make them in under 30 minutes to improve your health and lose weight

99

Sweet Potato Enchilada Bowls

Nutritional Values Per Serving

Calories	414
Total Fat	3.1g
Saturated Fat	0.5g
Cholesterol	0mg
Sodium	284mg
Total Carbohydrate	84.3g
Dietary Fiber	8.3g
Total Sugars	5.1g
Protein	13.2g

 Servings
4

 Preparation Time
10 minutes

Cooking Time
30 minutes

Ingredients:

- 2 teaspoons olive oil
- ½ yellow onion, diced
- 1 red pepper, diced
- 1 green pepper, diced
- 1 sweet potato, peeled and spiralized
- 1 cup corn kernels
- 1 (15 ounces.) can black beans, drained
- 1 teaspoon cumin
- 1 teaspoon paprika
- 1 teaspoon granulated garlic
- ½ teaspoon salt
- 2 cups enchilada sauce
- 2 cups cooked rice

Gluten-Free Enchiladas Sauce

- 1 teaspoon vegetable shortening
- 4 garlic cloves, minced
- ½ cup vegetable broth
- 15 ounces tomato sauce
- 2 tablespoons chili powder
- 2 teaspoons dried oregano
- 2 teaspoons cumin
- 1 teaspoon onion powder
- ½ teaspoon sea salt
- ¼ teaspoon black pepper

Toppings

- ¼ cup diced avocado
- ¼ cup tomato, chopped
- ¼ cup cilantro, chopped
- ¼ cup salsa

Instructions:

1. For enchilada sauce, sauté garlic with vegetable shortening in a saucepan for 1 minute.
2. Stir in broth, tomato sauce, chili powder, dried oregano, cumin, onion powder, salt and black pepper.
3. Mix well and cook on a simmer for 10 minutes with occasional stirring. Keep this sauce aside.
4. Sauté yellow onion with olive oil in a large cooking pan for 2 minutes.
5. Stir in sweet potatoes and peppers, then sauté for 10 minutes.
6. Add all the spices, corn and black beans, then cook for 2 minutes.
7. Stir in enchilada sauce and cook for 5 minutes.
8. Divide cooked rice into the serving bowls and add the beans mixture on top.
9. Garnish with avocado, tomato, cilantro and salsa.
10. Serve.

Storage Tips:

Place this enchilada meal in a sealable container and refrigerate for no more than 2 days.

 100

The 30-Minute Gluten-free Vegan Cookbook for Beginners
150 simple, delicious, and nutritious whole food, plant-based, and Gluten-free recipes. Make them in under 30 minutes to improve your health and lose weight

Enchiladas with Cauliflower Rice

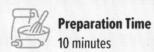 **Servings** 8

 Preparation Time 10 minutes

Cooking Time 26 minutes

Nutritional Values Per Serving

Calories	516
Total Fat	10.4g
Saturated Fat	4.4g
Cholesterol	15mg
Sodium	515mg
Total Carbohydrate	96g
Dietary Fiber	28.6g
Total Sugars	4.8g
Protein	25.8g

Ingredients:

Gluten-Free Enchiladas Sauce

- 1 teaspoon vegetable shortening
- 4 garlic cloves, minced
- ½ cup vegetable broth
- 15 ounces tomato sauce
- 2 tablespoons chili powder
- 2 teaspoons dried oregano
- 2 teaspoons cumin
- 1 teaspoon onion powder
- ½ teaspoon sea salt
- ¼ teaspoon black pepper

Enchiladas

- 2 teaspoons olive oil
- ½ small yellow onion, chopped
- 1 small green pepper, chopped
- 1 small red pepper, chopped
- 2 cups cauliflower rice
- 1 cup sweet corn kernels
- 1 (15 ounces.) can black beans, drained
- 2 teaspoons ground cumin
- 2 teaspoons paprika
- 1 teaspoon garlic powder
- 1 teaspoon salt
- ¼ teaspoon black pepper
- 8 corn tortillas, chopped
- 19 ounces gluten-free enchilada sauce
- 1 cup grated vegan cheese
- Cilantro for garnish

Instructions:

1. For enchilada sauce, sauté garlic with vegetable shortening in a saucepan for 1 minute.
2. Stir in broth, tomato sauce, chili powder, dried oregano, cumin, onion powder, salt and black pepper.
3. Mix well and cook on a simmer for 10 minutes with occasional stirring. Keep this sauce aside.
4. Sauté onion with oil in a large cooking pan for 2 minutes.
5. Stir in cauliflower rice and peppers, then cook for 5 minutes.
6. Add beans, spices, and corn.
7. Cook for 5 minutes, then divide this mixture into the corn tortillas.
8. Top the filling with enchilada sauce and vegan cheese and roll the tortillas.
9. Place them on a suitable baking sheet and broil for 3 minutes in the oven at 350 degrees F.
10. Garnish with cilantro.
11. Serve.

Storage Tips:

Transfer the enchiladas to a sealable container or a food-grade ziplock bag, seal it, and refrigerate it for no more than 2 days or freeze it for up to 3 months.

The 30-Minute Gluten-free Vegan Cookbook for Beginners
150 simple, delicious, and nutritious whole food, plant-based, and Gluten-free recipes. Make them in under 30 minutes to improve your health and lose weight

101

Zucchini Noodle Chickpea Bowls

Nutritional Values Per Serving

Calories	445
Total Fat	9.4g
Saturated Fat	1.2g
Cholesterol	0mg
Sodium	392mg
Total Carbohydrate	74.8g
Dietary Fiber	14g
Total Sugars	11.3g
Protein	18g

 Servings 6

 Preparation Time 10 minutes

 Cooking Time 15 minutes

Ingredients:

- 2 large zucchinis
- 1 (15 ounces) can of chickpeas, rinsed
- 1 cup rice, cooked
- 2 tablespoons olive oil
- Salt, to taste
- Sesame seeds, for garnish
- Chopped green onion for garnish

Orange Ginger Sauce

- ½ cup orange juice
- ¼ cup water
- 2 tablespoons tamari
- 1 tablespoon toasted sesame oil
- 1 garlic clove, grated
- ½ teaspoon fresh ginger, grated
- 1½ teaspoons corn starch

Instructions:

1. Mix all the orange ginger sauce ingredients in a bowl.
2. Pass zucchini through a spiralizer to get zucchini noodles.
3. Sauté spiralized zucchini with oil and a pinch of salt in a large skillet for 5 minutes.
4. Stir in chickpeas, and the prepared orange sauce, then cook for 10 minutes.
5. Divide the rice into 4 serving portions and top each portion with ¼ of the zucchini and chickpea mixture.
6. Garnish with green onion and sesame seeds.
7. Enjoy.

Serving Suggestion:

Serve these bowls with boiled white rice on the side.

Storage Tips:

Transfer this chickpea meal to a food-grade plastic bag, flatten this bag and refrigerate for no more than 2 days, or you can freeze it for up to 3 months.

 102

Quinoa Chili

Nutritional Values Per Serving

Calories	355
Total Fat	7.9g
Saturated Fat	1.1g
Cholesterol	0mg
Sodium	104mg
Total Carbohydrate	58.2g
Dietary Fiber	12.1g
Total Sugars	6g
Protein	16.8g

 Servings 4

 Preparation Time 10 minutes

 Cooking Time 30 minutes

Ingredients:

- ½ cup quinoa
- 1 cup vegetable stock
- ½ green pepper, seeded and sliced
- 1 red chili, seeded and sliced
- 1 small yellow onion, chopped
- 1 garlic clove, peeled and chopped
- 1 ½ tablespoon olive oil
- 2 ½ tablespoons tomato paste
- 1 (14 ounces) can of chopped tomatoes
- 1 cup corn
- 1 (7 ounces) can of kidney beans, rinsed
- 1 tablespoon lime juice
- 1 pinch of sea salt
- 1 pinch of white pepper
- 1 teaspoon chili powder
- 1 pinch of dried oregano
- 1 pinch of ground cumin
- 1 teaspoon maple syrup

Instructions:

1. Rinse the quinoa under water and add to a cooking pot.
2. Pour in vegetable stock, then cook for 15 minutes on medium-high heat and drain.
3. Strain the cooked quinoa and keep it aside.
4. Sauté onion, green pepper, garlic and red chili with oil in a large cooking pot for 5 minutes.
5. Stir in tomatoes and cook for 5 minutes.
6. Add corn, kidney beans, tomato paste and quinoa, then cook for 5 minutes.
7. Stir in lime juice, salt, white pepper, chili powder, cumin, maple syrup and oregano.
8. Mix well and serve.

Serving Suggestion:

Enjoy this quinoa chili with vegan fried rice.

Storage Tips:

Keep the quinoa chili in a sealable container and refrigerate for no more than 2 days or freeze it for up to 3 months.

The 30-Minute Gluten-free Vegan Cookbook for Beginners
150 simple, delicious, and nutritious whole food, plant-based, and Gluten-free recipes. Make them in under 30 minutes to improve your health and lose weight

103

Taco Rice Bowls

Nutritional Values Per Serving	
Calories	318
Total Fat	15.8g
Saturated Fat	2.8g
Cholesterol	0mg
Sodium	308mg
Total Carbohydrate	41.9g
Dietary Fiber	8.3g
Total Sugars	4.4g
Protein	6.6g

 Servings
6

 Preparation Time
10 minutes

 Cooking Time
10 minutes

Ingredients:

- 2 tablespoons olive oil
- 1 yellow onion, chopped
- 1 ½ cups of corn
- 3 cups cooked brown rice
- 1 (14 ounces.) can black beans, rinsed
- 1 tablespoon chili powder

- 1 teaspoon dried oregano
- ½ teaspoon salt
- 2 tomatoes, chopped
- ¼ cup salsa
- ½ cup fresh cilantro, chopped

Garnish

- 2 avocados, diced
- 2 cups romaine lettuce, shredded
- ½ cup fresh cilantro, chopped

Instructions:

1. Sauté onion with oil in a large skillet over medium heat for 2 minutes.
2. Stir in corn kernels and cook for 3 minutes.
3. Add brown rice, black beans, chili powder, salt and oregano.
4. Cook for 5 minutes, then add chopped tomatoes, salsa, and cilantro.
5. Mix well and transfer to a bowl.
6. Garnish with lettuce, avocado and cilantro.
7. Serve.

Storage Tips:

Pack the taco rice bowls in a small ziplock bag or reaction-free container and refrigerate for no more than 3 days or you can freeze it for 3 months.

The 30-Minute Gluten-free Vegan Cookbook for Beginners
150 simple, delicious, and nutritious whole food, plant-based, and Gluten-free recipes. Make them in under 30 minutes to improve your health and lose weight

Fried Rice with Tofu

Nutritional Values Per Serving	
Calories	337
Total Fat	9.6g
Saturated Fat	1.2g
Cholesterol	0mg
Sodium	1481mg
Total Carbohydrate	53.8g
Dietary Fiber	6.2g
Total Sugars	6.6g
Protein	12.1g

 Servings 2

 Preparation Time 15 minutes

 Cooking Time 10 minutes

Ingredients:

Tofu

- 1 (12 ounces) block of extra firm tofu, pressed
- 2 tablespoons cornstarch
- 1 teaspoon grated fresh ginger
- 3 garlic cloves, pressed
- 2 tablespoons tamari
- 2 tablespoons olive oil

Fried Rice

- 2 teaspoons grated fresh ginger
- 3 garlic cloves, minced
- 2 tablespoons toasted sesame oil
- 1 large head of broccoli, cut into florets
- 1 small yellow onion, chopped
- 4 carrots, peeled and sliced
- 8 white mushrooms, sliced
- ¼ cup tamari
- 4 cups brown rice, cooked

Instructions:

1. Cut the pressed tofu into cubes and mix them with cornstarch in a bowl.
2. Mix ginger, garlic cloves and tamari in another bowl.
3. Add olive oil to a large skillet and heat it over medium heat.
4. Sear the coated tofu cubes for 1 minute per side until golden brown.
5. Pour in ginger tamari mixture and mix well, then transfer to a bowl.
6. Sauté ginger and garlic cloves with sesame oil in the same skillet for 1 minute.
7. Toss in carrots and broccoli, then cook for 2 minutes.
8. Stir in onion and sauté for 2 minutes.
9. Toss in mushrooms and cook for 2 minutes.
10. Toss in the cooked tofu, brown rice and remaining tamari.
11. Mix all the ingredients with brown rice well.
12. Serve warm.

Storage Tips:

Keep the fried rice with tofu in a sealable glass container and refrigerate for no more than 3 days. Reheat in the microwave before serving.

The 30-Minute Gluten-free Vegan Cookbook for Beginners
150 simple, delicious, and nutritious whole food, plant-based, and Gluten-free recipes. Make them in under 30 minutes to improve your health and lose weight

105

Brussels Sprouts Curry

Nutritional Values Per Serving	
Calories	279
Total Fat	19.6g
Saturated Fat	13.4g
Cholesterol	0mg
Sodium	327mg
Total Carbohydrate	24.4g
Dietary Fiber	4.3g
Total Sugars	3.6g
Protein	5g

 Servings
4

 Preparation Time
10 minutes

 Cooking Time
15 minutes

Ingredients:

- 1 teaspoon sesame oil
- 3 garlic cloves, peeled and chopped
- 1 ginger 1-inch piece, chopped
- 1 small Thai chili pepper, chopped
- 1 medium onion, diced

- 1 medium carrot, sliced
- 1 medium potato, diced
- ½ lb. Brussels sprouts halved
- 1 (13 ½ ounce) can of coconut milk
- 2 tablespoons tahini
- 1 teaspoon turmeric
- 1 tablespoon rice vinegar

- 1 tablespoon agave
- 1 tablespoon tamari
- ½ teaspoon salt
- ¼ teaspoon black pepper
- ¼ cup sesame seeds toasted
- ¼ cup cilantro, chopped
- 1 teaspoon sesame oil

Instructions:

1. Sauté onion with garlic, ginger, chili pepper and oil in a large skillet for 3 minutes.
2. Stir in potato, carrot, brussels sprouts, coconut milk, tahini, turmeric, rice vinegar, agave, tamari, salt and black pepper, then cook for 10 minutes on a simmer.
3. Meanwhile, toast the sesame seeds in a small dry skillet until golden brown.
4. Garnish the curry with sesame seeds, sesame oil and cilantro.
5. Serve warm.

Storage Tips:

Keep this Brussel sprouts curry in a sealable storage container and refrigerate for no more than 2 days, or you can freeze it for up to 3 months. Reheat it at medium-low temperature before serving.

The 30-Minute Gluten-free Vegan Cookbook for Beginners
150 simple, delicious, and nutritious whole food, plant-based, and Gluten-free recipes. Make them in under 30 minutes to improve your health and lose weight

Korean Potato Curry

Nutritional Values Per Serving	
Calories	200
Total Fat	1.7g
Saturated Fat	0.4g
Cholesterol	0mg
Sodium	835mg
Total Carbohydrate	40.5g
Dietary Fiber	6.3g
Total Sugars	13.7g
Protein	9.3g

 Servings
4

 Preparation Time
10 minutes

 Cooking Time
15 minutes

Ingredients:

- 4 yellow potatoes, peeled and diced
- 3 carrots, chopped
- 1 red bell pepper, chopped
- 1 green bell pepper, chopped
- 1 green apple, diced
- 4 cups vegetable broth
- 1 yellow onion, chopped
- 2 cups mushrooms, sliced
- 3 cubes curry block, gluten-free

Instructions:

1. Sauté chopped bell peppers, onion and mushrooms in a large pan for 5 minutes.
2. Stir in potatoes, carrots, green apple and vegetable broth.
3. Cook this mixture to a boil, then cook for 10 minutes.
4. Stir in curry blocks, mix and cook until they dissolve.
5. Serve.

Serving Suggestion:

Enjoy this curry with boiled rice or with a gluten-free flatbread.

Storage Tips:

This Korean potato curry can be best stored in a refrigerator for no more than 2 days or in a freezer for up to 3 months. To do so, pack it in a small ziplock bag or reaction-free container.

The 30-Minute Gluten-free Vegan Cookbook for Beginners
150 simple, delicious, and nutritious whole food, plant-based, and Gluten-free recipes. Make them in under 30 minutes to improve your health and lose weight

107

CHAPTER 07

SNACKS, SALADS, AND SANDWICHES

Gluten-free
Vegan Salad Recipes

Winter Squash Salad with Kale

Nutritional Values Per Serving	
Calories	152
Total Fat	7.2g
Saturated Fat	0.9g
Cholesterol	0mg
Sodium	91mg
Total Carbohydrate	19.4g
Dietary Fiber	3.6g
Total Sugars	6.6g
Protein	3.6g

Servings 4

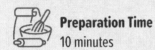 **Preparation Time** 10 minutes

 **Cooking Time** 25 minutes

Ingredients:

- 1 delicata squash, seeds removed and sliced
- 1 tablespoon avocado oil
- 6 cups kale, chopped
- 1 pinch of salt
- 1 tablespoon olive oil
- ¾ cup fennel, sliced
- 1 apple, cut into matchsticks
- ½ cup roasted pepitas (pumpkin seeds)
- 1 avocado, sliced

Instructions:

1. Preheat your oven to 450 degrees F.
2. Toss squash slices with avocado oil in a bowl and spread on a suitable baking sheet.
3. Now bake the squash in the preheated oven for 25 minutes and flip the slices once cooked halfway through.
4. Add chopped kale, olive oil, and a pinch of salt to a salad bowl.
5. Stir in apple, fennel, baked squash, avocado, and pepitas.
6. Serve.

Serving Suggestion:

Enjoy this salad with chopped pecans and vegan feta on top.

Storage Tips:

This winter squash salad can be best stored in a refrigerator for no more than 2 days, and to do so, pack it in a small ziplock bag or reaction-free container.

Roasted Sweet Potato Salad

Nutritional Values Per Serving	
Calories	157
Total Fat	6.1g
Saturated Fat	0.8g
Cholesterol	0mg
Sodium	207mg
Total Carbohydrate	25.8g
Dietary Fiber	3.6g
Total Sugars	18.5g
Protein	3g

 Servings 4

 Preparation Time 10 minutes

 Cooking Time 26 minutes

Ingredients:

Salad

- 1 bunch kale, well cleaned and ribs removed
- 2 ½ lbs sweet potatoes, peeled and diced
- Salt and black pepper to taste
- 1 tablespoon olive oil
- 1 shallot, sliced
- 3 tablespoons slivered almonds

Lemon Vinaigrette

- ¼ cup olive oil
- 2 tablespoons lemon juice
- 3 tablespoons maple syrup
- 1 garlic clove, chopped
- 1 ¼ teaspoon dried organic rosemary
- Salt and black pepper to taste

Instructions:

1. Preheat your oven to 450 degrees F.
2. Toss sweet potatoes with a pinch of salt, black pepper, and olive oil on a baking sheet.
3. Bake the sweet potatoes for 20 minutes, then add kale around the sweet potatoes.
4. Continue baking the veggies for 5 minutes.
5. Meanwhile, mix the lemon vinaigrette in a salad bowl.
6. Toast almonds in a dry skillet for 1 minute.
7. Add these almonds, sweet potatoes, shallot, and kale to the vinaigrette in the salad bowl.
8. Mix the veggies well with the vinaigrette.
9. Serve.

Serving Suggestion:

Drizzle olive oil or apple cider vinegar over the salad before serving.

Storage Tips:

This salad can be best stored in a refrigerator for no more than 2 days, and to do so, pack it in a small ziplock bag or reaction-free container.

The 30-Minute Gluten-free Vegan Cookbook for Beginners
150 simple, delicious, and nutritious whole food, plant-based, and Gluten-free recipes. Make them in under 30 minutes to improve your health and lose weight

111

Red Cabbage Cranberry Salad

Nutritional Values Per Serving	
Calories	178
Total Fat	11.1g
Saturated Fat	1.1g
Cholesterol	0mg
Sodium	41mg
Total Carbohydrate	19.1g
Dietary Fiber	5.1g
Total Sugars	11.9g
Protein	3.8g

 Servings 6

 Preparation Time 10 minutes

 Cooking Time 2 minutes

Ingredients:

- ½ red cabbage, shredded
- 2 apples, diced
- 1 small red onion, chopped
- 2 ounces dried cranberries
- ½ cup walnuts, broken into small pieces

Dressing

- 2 tablespoons olive oil
- 1 tablespoon walnut oil
- 1 tablespoon rice wine vinegar
- ½ teaspoon Dijon mustard

Instructions:

1. Toast walnuts in a dry pan for 2 minutes over high heat, then transfer to a bowl.
2. Toss shredded cabbage with apple, red onion, and dried cranberries in a salad bowl.
3. Mix walnut oil, olive oil, rice wine vinegar, and Dijon mustard in a bowl.
4. Add this dressing and the toasted nuts to the salad then mix well.
5. Serve.

Serving Suggestion:

Sprinkle pomegranate seeds over the salad before serving.

Storage Tips:

Put the salad into a sealable container and refrigerate for no more than 2 days. Make sure not to add apples to the salad until you are ready to serve it.

The 30-Minute Gluten-free Vegan Cookbook for Beginners
150 simple, delicious, and nutritious whole food, plant-based, and Gluten-free recipes. Make them in under 30 minutes to improve your health and lose weight

Pomelo Rice Noodle Salad

Nutritional Values Per Serving	
Calories	359
Total Fat	7.5g
Saturated Fat	1g
Cholesterol	0mg
Sodium	40mg
Total Carbohydrate	69.3g
Dietary Fiber	5.8g
Total Sugars	24.4g
Protein	6.7g

 Servings 4

 Preparation Time 15 minutes

 Cooking Time 15 minutes

Ingredients:

Marinade

- 5 tablespoons rice wine vinegar
- ¼ cup brown rice syrup
- 1 tablespoon orange blossom water
- 2-star anise pods
- 2 cinnamon sticks
- 1 piece of fresh ginger, cut into strips
- 1 red chili, cut into thin strips

Salad

- 2 cups rice noodles
- 1 large pomelo
- 1 mango, peeled and cut into strips
- ½ cup cilantro leaves
- ⅓ cup mint leaves
- 1 red shallot, sliced
- 1 teaspoon sesame oil
- Juice of one lime
- 2 teaspoon black sesame seeds
- ¼ cup raw peanuts, chopped
- Sprinkle of salt

Instructions:

1. Mix vinegar with brown rice syrup in a small saucepan and cook until it's just heated then remove it from the heat.
2. Stir in orange blossom water, cinnamon, star anise, ginger, and chili.
3. Peel and divide the pomelo segments, then squeeze the juice of two chunks of pomelo into the vinegar dressing, then leave for 30 minutes.
4. Meanwhile, boil the rice noodles as per the package's instructions, then drain and allow them to cool.
5. Remove the star anise, cinnamon, and ginger from the dressing.
6. Now add the remaining pomelo, the prepared dressing, cooked noodles, mango, and the rest of the ingredients to a salad bowl.
7. Mix gently and serve.

Serving Suggestion:

Garnish this salad with toasted sesame seeds before serving.

Storage Tips:

Transfer the salad to a sealable container or a food-grade ziplock bag, seal it, and refrigerate it for no more than 2 days or freeze it for up to 3 months.

The 30-Minute Gluten-free Vegan Cookbook for Beginners
150 simple, delicious, and nutritious whole food, plant-based, and Gluten-free recipes. Make them in under 30 minutes to improve your health and lose weight

113

Carrot Black Bean Salad

Nutritional Values Per Serving	
Calories	491
Total Fat	14.6g
Saturated Fat	2.9g
Cholesterol	0mg
Sodium	117mg
Total Carbohydrate	76.1g
Dietary Fiber	20.9g
Total Sugars	17.1g
Protein	19.2g

 Servings
4

 Preparation Time
10 minutes

Cooking Time
30 minutes

Ingredients:

Salad

- 10 carrots, peeled
- 1 teaspoon cumin seeds, crushed
- 1 ½ teaspoon coriander seeds, crushed
- 1 tablespoon olive oil
- 1 ½ cups cooked black beans

- ½ ounce parsley, chopped
- ½ ounce mint, chopped
- ½ ounce coriander, chopped
- ½ small red onion, diced
- 1 medium avocado, sliced
- Salt and black pepper to taste

Orange cinnamon dressing

- Zest of 1 large orange
- 3 tablespoons olive oil
- 2 tablespoons lemon juice
- 1 small garlic clove, minced
- ¼ teaspoon cinnamon
- Salt and black pepper to taste

Instructions:

1. Preheat your oven to 400 degrees F.
2. Spread parchment paper on a baking sheet.
3. Toss carrots with 1 tablespoon olive oil, cumin, coriander seeds, a pinch of salt, and a pinch of black pepper in a bowl and spread them on the baking sheet.
4. Bake the carrots for 30 minutes in the preheated oven.
5. Mix the roasted carrots with the rest of the salad and dressing ingredients in a salad bowl.
6. Serve.

Serving Suggestion:

Serve this salad with chopped pecans on top.

Storage Tips:

Transfer the bean salad to a food-grade plastic bag, remove all the air and seal the bag, then refrigerate for no more than 2 days or you can freeze it for up to 3 months.

Quinoa Salad

Nutritional Values Per Serving

Calories	389
Total Fat	17g
Saturated Fat	2.5g
Cholesterol	0mg
Sodium	63mg
Total Carbohydrate	50.8g
Dietary Fiber	6.6g
Total Sugars	5.4g
Protein	11g

 Servings 4

 Preparation Time 10 minutes

 Cooking Time 25 minutes

Ingredients:

Quinoa

- 4 cups vegetable broth
- 1 ½ cups raw whole-grain quinoa
- Salt, to taste

Vinaigrette

- ⅓ cup lemon juice
- ¼ cup olive oil
- 2 garlic cloves, minced
- Salt, to taste
- Black pepper, to taste

Vegetables

- 1 medium cucumber, chopped
- 1 red bell pepper, chopped
- ½ small red onion, chopped
- ½ cup broccoli florets, steamed and chopped
- 2 medium tomatoes, chopped

Instructions:

1. Boil vegetable broth with 1 teaspoon salt in a medium saucepan.
2. Add quinoa and cook for 20 minutes, then strain and rinse.
3. Mix quinoa with lemon juice, oil, garlic, salt, and black pepper in a salad bowl.
4. Stir in the rest of the vegetables and mix well.
5. Serve.

Serving Suggestion:

Serve this salad over a lettuce bed.

Storage Tips:

Keep the salad in a sealable container and refrigerate for no more than 2 days or freeze it for up to 3 months.

The 30-Minute Gluten-free Vegan Cookbook for Beginners
150 simple, delicious, and nutritious whole food, plant-based, and Gluten-free recipes. Make them in under 30 minutes to improve your health and lose weight

115

Cucumber Salad

Nutritional Values Per Serving

Calories	111
Total Fat	5g
Saturated Fat	0.7g
Cholesterol	0mg
Sodium	546mg
Total Carbohydrate	13.4g
Dietary Fiber	2.2g
Total Sugars	7.3g
Protein	1.9g

 Servings 4

 Preparation Time 10 minutes

 Cooking Time 0 minutes

Ingredients:

- 1½ pounds cucumbers, cut into chunks
- ½ teaspoon salt
- 4 scallions, sliced
- 1 teaspoon ginger, grated
- 1 garlic clove, minced
- ¼ cup rice vinegar
- 1 tablespoon tamari
- 1 tablespoon sesame oil
- 1 tablespoon maple syrup
- 1 teaspoon red chili paste
- 2 tablespoons toasted sesame seeds

Instructions:

1. Place cucumbers in a colander and sprinkle a pinch of salt over them.
2. Leave the cucumbers for 10 minutes to release some of their water.
3. Meanwhile, mix scallions, remaining salt, and the rest of the ingredients in a salad bowl.
4. Stir in cucumber and mix well to coat.
5. Serve.

Serving Suggestion:

Serve this salad alongside some quinoa chili.

Storage Tips:

Do not store this salad in the refrigerator for more than a day.

Fennel Asparagus Salad

Nutritional Values Per Serving	
Calories	264
Total Fat	25.5g
Saturated Fat	3.8g
Cholesterol	0mg
Sodium	373mg
Total Carbohydrate	10.8g
Dietary Fiber	5.4g
Total Sugars	1.8g
Protein	2.4g

 Servings 4

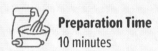 **Preparation Time** 10 minutes

 **Cooking Time** 11 minutes

Ingredients:

- 1 large leek, chopped
- ⅓ cup olive oil
- 1 large fennel bulb, chopped
- 6 large asparagus stalks, chopped
- 1 tablespoon lemon thyme
- 2 tablespoons lemon juice
- ¾ teaspoon salt
- ½ teaspoon black pepper
- 1 teaspoon ground coriander
- ¼ cup almonds, lightly toasted
- 1 avocado, sliced

Instructions:

1. Sauté leek with 3 tablespoons of oil in a sauté pan for 6 minutes.
2. Add fennel bulb, asparagus, and a pinch of salt, then sauté for 5 minutes.
3. Transfer this mixture to a salad bowl.
4. Add lemon thyme, lemon juice, salt, black pepper, remaining oil, and coriander.
5. Toss well to coat, then garnish with almonds and avocado.
6. Enjoy.

Serving Suggestion:

Serve this salad alongside some brussels sprout curry.

Storage Tips:

Keep the salad in a sealable glass container and refrigerate for no more than 3 days. Reheat in the microwave before serving.

The 30-Minute Gluten-free Vegan Cookbook for Beginners
150 simple, delicious, and nutritious whole food, plant-based, and Gluten-free recipes. Make them in under 30 minutes to improve your health and lose weight

117

Potato Salad with Peas

Nutritional Values Per Serving	
Calories	304
Total Fat	17.7g
Saturated Fat	2.6g
Cholesterol	0mg
Sodium	404mg
Total Carbohydrate	32.6g
Dietary Fiber	7g
Total Sugars	5.9g
Protein	7.4g

 Servings 4

 Preparation Time 10 minutes

Cooking Time 18 minutes

Ingredients:

- 1 lb. fingerling potatoes, peeled and diced
- 2 cups fresh English peas
- ½ cup chopped celery
- 1 cup Italian parsley, chopped
- ¼ cup tarragon leaves, chopped
- 4 scallions, chopped
- 1 garlic clove, minced
- ⅓ cup olive oil
- Zest from 1 lemon
- ½ teaspoon salt
- ½ teaspoon black pepper
- 1 tablespoon whole-grain mustard
- 1 tablespoon capers

Instructions:

1. Half-fill a large cooking pot with water and bring to a boil. Add potatoes.
2. Cook for 18 minutes, then add peas and cook for 2 minutes, then drain out the water.
3. Allow the potatoes to cool, then cut them in half.
4. Mix the potatoes with peas, celery, and the rest of the ingredients in a salad bowl.
5. Serve.

Serving Suggestion:

Garnish this salad with crushed nuts on top.

Storage Tips:

Keep this potato salad in a sealable storage container and refrigerate for no more than 2 days, or you can freeze it for up to 3 months. Defrost at room temperature to serve again.

The 30-Minute Gluten-free Vegan Cookbook for Beginners
150 simple, delicious, and nutritious whole food, plant-based, and Gluten-free recipes. Make them in under 30 minutes to improve your health and lose weight

Beetroot Salad with Pistachios

 Servings
6

 Preparation Time
10 minutes

Cooking Time
15 minutes

Nutritional Values Per Serving	
Calories	237
Total Fat	19.4g
Saturated Fat	5.6g
Cholesterol	22mg
Sodium	560mg
Total Carbohydrate	12.5g
Dietary Fiber	2.7g
Total Sugars	8.4g
Protein	6.7g

Ingredients:

- 1½ lbs. beets, peeled and diced
- ⅓ cup red onion, chopped
- 1 garlic clove, minced
- 4 tablespoons olive oil
- 2 tablespoons red wine vinegar
- 2 tablespoons orange zest
- 4 tablespoons orange juice
- 1 cup craisins
- ½ teaspoon salt
- ½ teaspoon black pepper
- 1 cup cilantro, chopped
- 1 cup pistachios, chopped
- 1 cup vegan feta, cut into cubes

Garnish

- ¼ cup pomegranate seeds

Instructions:

1. Add beets to a large cooking pot and pour in enough water to cover them.
2. Bring the beets to a boil, then continue to cook for 10-15 minutes until tender.
3. Drain and transfer the beets to a salad bowl, then allow them to cool.
4. Add onion, garlic, olive oil, orange juice and zest, vinegar, black pepper, salt, craisins, cilantro, feta, and pistachios.
5. Mix well and garnish with pomegranate seeds.
6. Serve.

Serving Suggestion:

Enjoy this salad with a pulled mushroom BBQ sandwich.

Storage Tips:

This salad can be best stored in a refrigerator for no more than 2 days or in a freezer for up to 3 months. To do so, pack it in a small ziplock bag or reaction-free container.

The 30-Minute Gluten-free Vegan Cookbook for Beginners
150 simple, delicious, and nutritious whole food, plant-based, and Gluten-free recipes. Make them in under 30 minutes to improve your health and lose weight

119

Gluten-free
Vegan Snacks

Peanut Butter Energy Bites

 Servings
6

 Preparation Time
30 minutes

 Cooking Time
0 minutes

Nutritional Values Per Serving	
Calories	340
Total Fat	19g
Saturated Fat	6.4g
Cholesterol	5mg
Sodium	18mg
Total Carbohydrate	31.9g
Dietary Fiber	6g
Total Sugars	15g
Protein	10.8g

Ingredients:

- 1 cup rolled oats
- ⅔ cup shredded coconut
- ½ cup natural peanut butter
- ½ cup ground flax seed
- ½ cup dark chocolate chips
- ⅓ cup maple syrup
- 1 tablespoon chia seeds
- 1 teaspoon vanilla

Instructions:

1. Blend oats with coconut, peanut butter, flaxseeds, chocolate chips, maple, chia seeds, and vanilla in a food processor for 2 minutes.
2. Make 1-inch balls out of this mixture and place them on a baking sheet.
3. Refrigerate these balls for 20 minutes.
4. Serve.

Serving Suggestion:

Roll these energy bites in coconut shreds for taste.

Storage Tips:

Add these bites to a sealable container, store them at room temperature for 2-3 days, refrigerate for a week or freeze them for up to 6 months.

The 30-Minute Gluten-free Vegan Cookbook for Beginners
150 simple, delicious, and nutritious whole food, plant-based, and Gluten-free recipes. Make them in under 30 minutes to improve your health and lose weight

121

Crunchy Kale Chips

Nutritional Values Per Serving	
Calories	57
Total Fat	4.7g
Saturated Fat	0.7g
Cholesterol	0mg
Sodium	15mq
Total Carbohydrate	3.6g
Dietary Fiber	0.5g
Total Sugars	0g
Protein	1g

 Servings 2

 Preparation Time 10 minutes

 Cooking Time 20 minutes

Ingredients:

- 1 bunch of kale, leaves separated, washed
- 2 teaspoons olive oil
- 1 pinch salt
- 1 pinch of garlic powder

Instructions:

1. Preheat your oven to 300 degrees F.
2. Rub the oil over the kale leaves.
3. Spread the oiled kale leaves on a baking sheet and sprinkle salt and garlic powder over them.
4. Bake the kale leaves for 10 minutes, then toss and continue baking for 10 minutes
5. Serve.

Serving Suggestion:

Sprinkle lemon juice over the kale before baking for a lemony taste.

Storage Tips:

You can store the chips in a food-grade ziplock plastic bag. Remove the air and seal the bag. Refrigerate for no more than 3 days or freeze it for up to 3 months.

Coconut Macaroons

 Servings
24

 Preparation Time
15 minutes

 Cooking Time
25 minutes

Nutritional Values Per Serving	
Calories	179
Total Fat	12.6g
Saturated Fat	10.7g
Cholesterol	0mg
Sodium	21mg
Total Carbohydrate	15.8g
Dietary Fiber	3g
Total Sugars	12.8g
Protein	2.6g

Ingredients:

- ¾ cup full-fat coconut milk
- 14 ounces sweetened coconut flakes
- ½ cup almond flour
- 1 teaspoon pure vanilla extract
- ½ teaspoon almond extract
- ¼ teaspoon salt

Aquafaba

- 4 tablespoons whipped aquafaba
- ¼ teaspoon cream of tartar

Chocolate dip

- 8 ounces dairy-free chocolate chips, melted

Instructions:

1. Preheat your oven to 325 degrees F.
2. Line two cookie sheets with parchment paper.
3. Beat whipped aquafaba with cream of tartar in a stand mixer until foamy.
4. Stir in coconut milk, coconut flakes, almond flour, salt, almond, and vanilla extract then mix well with a spatula just until combined.
5. Use a small scoop to make golf-ball-sized balls out of this mixture.
6. Place each scoop onto the cookie sheets while keeping a 3 inches distance between them.
7. Bake the macaroons for 25 minutes in the preheated oven.
8. Allow the macaroons to cool, then dip them in the melted chocolate.
9. Place the macaroons on the parchment paper with their chocolate side upward and leave them for 5 minutes to set.
10. Serve.

Storage Tips:

Store the macaroon in a cookie jar for 3 days or refrigerate in a sealed container for a week or two.

The 30-Minute Gluten-free Vegan Cookbook for Beginners
150 simple, delicious, and nutritious whole food, plant-based, and Gluten-free recipes. Make them in under 30 minutes to improve your health and lose weight

123

Oven Fries

Nutritional Values Per Serving

Calories	200
Total Fat	6.5g
Saturated Fat	1g
Cholesterol	0mg
Sodium	21mg
Total Carbohydrate	32.2g
Dietary Fiber	3.5g
Total Sugars	1.6g
Protein	4g

 Servings
8

 Preparation Time
10 minutes

 Cooking Time
30 minutes

Ingredients:

- 2 pounds large russet potatoes
- 1/4 cup olive oil
- 2 teaspoons gluten-free Italian seasoning blend
- Black pepper, to taste
- 1 teaspoon red pepper flakes

Instructions:

1. Preheat your oven to 425 degrees F.
2. Peel and cut the potatoes into ¼-inch fries.
3. Grease 13x9 inches baking dish with 1 tablespoon olive oil.
4. Toss the potato fries with the remaining oil and seasonings.
5. Spread the seasoned fries in the baking dish and bake for 15 minutes.
6. Toss and flip the fries and continue baking for 15 minutes until golden brown.
7. Serve.

Serving Suggestion:

Serve these fries with tomato sauce.

Storage Tips:

Freeze the uncooked fries in a ziplock bag and bake right before serving.

The 30-Minute Gluten-free Vegan Cookbook for Beginners
150 simple, delicious, and nutritious whole food, plant-based, and Gluten-free recipes. Make them in under 30 minutes to improve your health and lose weight

Vegan Stuffed Dates

Nutritional Values Per Serving	
Calories	139
Total Fat	9.1g
Saturated Fat	4.5g
Cholesterol	0mg
Sodium	122mg
Total Carbohydrate	13.8g
Dietary Fiber	1.4g
Total Sugars	10.5g
Protein	1.5g

 Servings
3

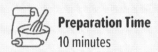 **Preparation Time**
10 minutes

 **Cooking Time**
0 minutes

Ingredients:

- 6 fresh Medjool dates
- 3 tablespoons vegan cream cheese
- 2 teaspoons dried dill

Instructions:

1. Mix cream cheese with dried dill in a small bowl.
2. Cut a slit in one side of the dates and remove the pits. Make sure not to cut them completely in half.
3. Take a small spoon and stuff the cream cheese into the dates.
4. Serve.

Serving Suggestion:

Drizzle chopped nuts over the dates to serve.

Storage Tips:

Keep the dates in a sealable container and refrigerate for 7-10 days or freeze for longer storage.

The 30-Minute Gluten-free Vegan Cookbook for Beginners
150 simple, delicious, and nutritious whole food, plant-based, and Gluten-free recipes. Make them in under 30 minutes to improve your health and lose weight

125

Oatmeal Bars

Nutritional Values Per Serving	
Calories	296
Total Fat	13.2g
Saturated Fat	2.6g
Cholesterol	0mg
Sodium	196mg
Total Carbohydrate	37.3g
Dietary Fiber	4.7g
Total Sugars	14.3g
Protein	10.1g

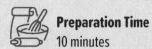 **Servings**
6

 **Preparation Time**
10 minutes

Cooking Time
2 minutes

Ingredients:

- 1 cup plus 2 tablespoons peanut butter
- ½ cup plus 2 tablespoons maple syrup
- 4 cups Old Fashioned rolled oats
- ½ teaspoon salt
- ½ teaspoon ground cinnamon

Instructions:

1. Blend oats with peanut butter, salt, maple syrup, and cinnamon in a food processor.
2. Line a 9x9 inches baking pan with parchment paper and spread the oats mixture on it.
3. Press the oats mixture into an even layer and freeze for 15 minutes.
4. Cut the oats mixture into 16 bars of equal size.
5. Serve.

Serving Suggestion:

Serve the bars with melted dark chocolate syrup on the side.

Storage Tips:

Pack these bars in a sealable container and store them at room temperature for 3-5 days or refrigerate for no more than 14 days or freeze for up to 3 months.

Roasted Chickpeas

 Servings
2

 Preparation Time
5 minutes

 Cooking Time
20 minutes

Nutritional Values Per Serving	
Calories	88
Total Fat	2g
Saturated Fat	0.2g
Cholesterol	0mg
Sodium	191mg
Total Carbohydrate	13.3g
Dietary Fiber	1.3g
Total Sugars	3g
Protein	5.3g

Ingredients:

- 1 cup canned chickpeas, rinsed
- ½ teaspoon olive oil
- 1 tablespoon nutritional yeast flakes
- 1 pinch salt

Instructions:

1. Preheat your oven to 400 degrees F.
2. Line a baking sheet with parchment paper.
3. Spread the chickpeas on the parchment paper.
4. Add oil, yeast flakes, and salt over them and toss well to coat.
5. Roast the seasoned chickpeas in the preheated oven for 20 minutes.
6. Serve.

Serving Suggestion:

Drizzle lemon juice over the chickpeas before serving.

Storage Tips:

You can store these chickpeas in a sealed container at room temperature in a dry and cool setting.

The 30-Minute Gluten-free Vegan Cookbook for Beginners
150 simple, delicious, and nutritious whole food, plant-based, and Gluten-free recipes. Make them in under 30 minutes to improve your health and lose weight

127

Brownie Bites

Nutritional Values Per Serving	
Calories	238
Total Fat	7.9g
Saturated Fat	2.4g
Cholesterol	0mg
Sodium	8mg
Total Carbohydrate	36.3g
Dietary Fiber	7g
Total Sugars	12g
Protein	7.9g

 Servings 6

 Preparation Time 5 minutes

 Cooking Time 0 minutes

Ingredients:

- ½ cup gluten-free oat flour
- ½ cup unsweetened cocoa powder
- ¼ cup ground flaxseed
- ½ cup vegan dark chocolate chips
- ¾ cup creamy almond butter
- ¼ cup pure maple syrup
- 1 teaspoon pure vanilla extract

Instructions:

1. Mix oat flour with cocoa powder, flaxseed, and chocolate chips in a bowl.
2. Stir in almond butter, maple syrup, and vanilla.
3. Mix well and make 1-inch balls out of this mixture using a small scoop.
4. Put these balls onto a baking sheet and refrigerate for 15 minutes.
5. Serve.

Serving Suggestion:

Drizzle melted dark chocolate chips over the brownie bites before serving.

Storage Tips:

Pack the brownie bites in a sealable container at room temperature for 1 week or in the refrigerator for a month.

 128

The 30-Minute Gluten-free Vegan Cookbook for Beginners
150 simple, delicious, and nutritious whole food, plant-based, and Gluten-free recipes. Make them in under 30 minutes to improve your health and lose weight

5 Ingredient Nut Bars

Nutritional Values Per Serving	
Calories	132
Total Fat	6.2g
Saturated Fat	0.6g
Cholesterol	0mg
Sodium	213mg
Total Carbohydrate	18.3g
Dietary Fiber	1.2g
Total Sugars	12.5g
Protein	2.6g

 Servings
4

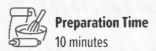 **Preparation Time**
10 minutes

 **Cooking Time**
30 minutes

Ingredients:

- 1 cup unsalted almonds, roasted
- ½ cup unsalted peanuts, roasted
- ½ cup vegan gluten-free brown rice crisp cereal
- ¼ teaspoon salt
- ¼ cup pure maple syrup

Instructions:

1. Preheat your oven to 350 degrees F.
2. Line a suitable 8-inch baking pan with parchment paper.
3. Toss almonds, peanuts, cereal, and salt together in a large bowl.
4. Add maple syrup and mix well to coat.
5. Spread this granola mixture in the baking pan, press down, and bake for 30 minutes.
6. Cut the granola into 12 bars and serve.

Storage Tips:

To preserve the flavors, you can keep them in a sealed container at room temperature for 7 days or store the bars in your refrigerator for a month.

The 30-Minute Gluten-free Vegan Cookbook for Beginners
150 simple, delicious, and nutritious whole food, plant-based, and Gluten-free recipes. Make them in under 30 minutes to improve your health and lose weight

129

No-Bake Cookies

Nutritional Values Per Serving	
Calories	249
Total Fat	10.7g
Saturated Fat	6.2g
Cholesterol	0mg
Sodium	90mg
Total Carbohydrate	35g
Dietary Fiber	2.9g
Total Sugars	20.3g
Protein	4g

 Servings 8

 Preparation Time 10 minutes

 Cooking Time 2 minutes

Ingredients:

- 3 ½ tablespoons coconut oil
- ½ cup almond butter
- ½ cup maple syrup
- ¼ teaspoon salt
- 1 ½ teaspoons vanilla extract

- 1 ½ cups rolled oats
- ½ teaspoon cinnamon
- 1 pinch of nutmeg
- ¾ cup raisins

Instructions:

1. Mix coconut oil with almond butter, maple syrup, and salt in a saucepan and cook, stirring constantly, for 2 minutes until it thickens.
2. Remove from the heat, then add vanilla extract.
3. Add nutmeg, cinnamon, raisins, and oats, then mix well.
4. Make 1-inch balls out of this mixture and press them into a cookie shape.
5. Serve.

Serving Suggestion:

Sprinkle cinnamon ground or drizzle melted chocolate chips over the cookies before serving.

Storage Tips:

Keep the cookies in a sealed cookie jar at room temperature.

The 30-Minute Gluten-free Vegan Cookbook for Beginners
150 simple, delicious, and nutritious whole food, plant-based, and Gluten-free recipes. Make them in under 30 minutes to improve your health and lose weight

Gluten-free
Vegan Sandwiches

Reuben Sandwiches

Nutritional Values Per Serving

Calories	192
Total Fat	10.3g
Saturated Fat	2g
Cholesterol	0mg
Sodium	633mg
Total Carbohydrate	28.9g
Dietary Fiber	5.3g
Total Sugars	3.3g
Protein	7.2g

 Servings
4

 Preparation Time
10 minutes

Cooking Time
0 minutes

Ingredients:

Cashew Cheese

- ½ cup unsalted cashews
- 1 tablespoon nutritional yeast
- 1/4 teaspoon garlic powder
- 2 teaspoons tahini
- 1 tablespoon Dijon mustard
- 2 tablespoons lemon juice
- ¼ cup water

Toppings

- 10 ounces sauerkraut, drained
- 4 basil leaves
- 4 spinach leaves
- 4 tomato slices
- 8 gluten-free pumpernickel bread slices

Instructions:

1. Blend cashews with yeast and garlic powder in a blender.
2. Add water, tahini, Dijon mustard and lemon juice, then blend until smooth.
3. Set a non-stick skillet over medium heat.
4. Place a bread slice in it and spread 2 tablespoons of cashew cheese over it.
5. Add ¼ spinach, sauerkraut, tomato and basil, then place the other bread slice on top.
6. Flip the spinach sandwich and toast the other side until golden brown.
7. Repeat the same with the remaining ingredients to make more sandwiches.
8. Serve.

Storage Tips:

Put the cooled leftover sandwiches into a sealable container, cover the lid and freeze for up to 3 months or refrigerate for no more than 2 days.

 132

Breadless Eggplant Sandwich

Nutritional Values Per Serving	
Calories	237
Total Fat	17.3g
Saturated Fat	3.4g
Cholesterol	0mg
Sodium	578mg
Total Carbohydrate	16.6g
Dietary Fiber	2g
Total Sugars	2.2g
Protein	7.5g

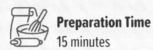 **Servings** 4

 **Preparation Time** 15 minutes

Cooking Time 20 minutes

Ingredients:

- 8 eggplant slices
- 1 cup cashews
- 4 cups hot boiling water
- 2 tablespoons tamari
- 2 teaspoons maple syrup
- 2 teaspoons olive oil
- 2 teaspoons white miso
- 1 teaspoon nutritional yeast
- 1 tablespoon red wine vinegar
- Sea salt, to taste
- 4 kale leaves
- 1 large tomato, sliced

Instructions:

1. Soak 1 cup of cashews in boiling water for 10 minutes, then drain.
2. Preheat your oven to 400 degrees F.
3. Line a baking tray with a foil sheet and grease it with 1 teaspoon of olive oil.
4. Place the eggplant slices on the baking tray.
5. Mix tamari with maple syrup and the other 1 teaspoon olive oil in a bowl.
6. Pour this mixture over the eggplant and bake for 20 minutes, then flip once cooked halfway through.
7. Meanwhile, blend cashews with yeast, miso, vinegar, and salt in a blender.
8. Spread the cashew cheese over half of the eggplant slices.
9. Top the slices with kale and tomato, then place the other slices on top to make sandwiches.
10. Serve.

Storage Tips:

Transfer the sandwiches to a food-grade plastic bag and vacuum seal it to store in your freezer.

The 30-Minute Gluten-free Vegan Cookbook for Beginners
150 simple, delicious, and nutritious whole food, plant-based, and Gluten-free recipes. Make them in under 30 minutes to improve your health and lose weight

133

Tofu Katsu Onigirazu Wrap

Nutritional Values Per Serving

Calories	393
Total Fat	31.2g
Saturated Fat	5.1g
Cholesterol	0mg
Sodium	23mg
Total Carbohydrate	25.1g
Dietary Fiber	3.8g
Total Sugars	2.8g
Protein	5.2g

 Servings 4

 Preparation Time 20 minutes

 Cooking Time 30 minutes

Ingredients:

Onigirazu

- 4 nori sheets
- 4 cups of cooked sushi rice
- 1 avocado, sliced
- 1-ounce baby spinach
- 1 red cabbage, shredded and pickled
- Sriracha or vegan mayo, to taste

Tofu Katsu

- 2 (7-ounce) packages firm tofu, pressed
- 1 tablespoon tamari
- 1 cup aquafaba (chickpea liquid)
- 2 cups gluten-free breadcrumbs
- 1 cup corn flour
- 1 tablespoon olive oil

Instructions:

1. Preheat your oven to 390 degrees F.
2. Line a suitable baking sheet with parchment paper and grease with 1 tablespoon of olive oil.
3. Coat tofu with tamari, then with corn flour.
4. Dip the tofu in aquafaba, then coat with gluten-free breadcrumbs.
5. Place the tofu katsu on the prepared baking sheet.
6. Bake the tofu for 30 minutes and flip once cooked halfway through.
7. Spread a nori sheet over a working surface.
8. Add ¼ of the rice on top of the nori sheet and spread it evenly while leaving ½ inch around the edges.
9. Put ¼ tofu, avocado, spinach, cabbage, and vegan mayo on top of the rice, at the center of nori sheet.
10. Roll the nori sheet into a wrap and repeat the same with the remaining steps.
11. Serve.

Serving Suggestion:

Serve the onigirazu with wasabi on the side.

Storage Tips:

Transfer this onigirazu to a food-grade plastic bag and vacuum seal it to store in your freezer.

The 30-Minute Gluten-free Vegan Cookbook for Beginners
150 simple, delicious, and nutritious whole food, plant-based, and Gluten-free recipes. Make them in under 30 minutes to improve your health and lose weight

Crispy Eggplant Pepper Wrap

 Servings
1

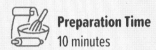 **Preparation Time**
10 minutes

 Cooking Time
10 minutes

Nutritional Values Per Serving	
Calories	691
Total Fat	46.1g
Saturated Fat	6.5g
Cholesterol	0mg
Sodium	671mg
Total Carbohydrate	69.1g
Dietary Fiber	17.7g
Total Sugars	23.7g
Protein	12.7g

Ingredients:

- 1 gluten-free corn tortilla wrap
- 6 thin slices of eggplant
- 2 tablespoons corn starch
- 1 pinch of salt
- 1 pinch of black pepper
- 3 tablespoons olive oil
- 1 handful of baby spinach leaves
- 2 tablespoons hummus
- 1 roasted red pepper, julienned

Instructions:

1. Mix cornstarch with black pepper and salt in a bowl.
2. Add eggplant slices and coat them well with the cornstarch mixture.
3. Set a large skillet over medium-high heat and add 3 tablespoons olive oil to heat.
4. Sear the eggplant for 5 minutes per side and transfer it to a cutting board.
5. Spread hummus over the corn tortilla then add eggplant.
6. Divide the rest of the ingredients over the eggplant slices and roll the wrap.
7. Serve.

Storage Tips:

To preserve the flavors, wrap this wrap with food-grade paper and refrigerate for 3 days or freeze for up to 3 months.

The 30-Minute Gluten-free Vegan Cookbook for Beginners
150 simple, delicious, and nutritious whole food, plant-based, and Gluten-free recipes. Make them in under 30 minutes to improve your health and lose weight

135

Hummus Veggie Wrap

Nutritional Values Per Serving

Calories	406
Total Fat	8.2g
Saturated Fat	1.6g
Cholesterol	0mg
Sodium	226mg
Total Carbohydrate	69g
Dietary Fiber	12.3g
Total Sugars	3.9g
Protein	15.3g

Servings
1

Preparation Time
10 minutes

Cooking Time
11 minutes

Ingredients:

- ¼ cup brown rice
- 1 gluten-free corn tortilla
- 2 tablespoons hummus
- 1 cup spinach
- ½ cup black beans, rinsed
- ½ medium carrot, sliced
- ¼ bell pepper, sliced
- ¼ cucumber, sliced
- ¼ avocado, sliced

Instructions:

1. Boil the brown rice as per the package's instructions.
2. Heat the tortilla in the microwave for 15 seconds.
3. Spread hummus over the tortilla and add rice, beans, spinach and the rest of the ingredients on top.
4. Roll the tortilla like a burrito and serve.

Storage Tips:

This wrap is best stored in a freezer, and to do so, pack it in a small ziplock bag or reaction-free container.

Avocado Chickpea Collard Wraps

Nutritional Values Per Serving

Calories	360
Total Fat	11.1g
Saturated Fat	1.9g
Cholesterol	0mg
Sodium	296mg
Total Carbohydrate	52.7g
Dietary Fiber	17.6g
Total Sugars	8.9g
Protein	15.9g

 Servings 6

 Preparation Time 10 minutes

Cooking Time 0 minutes

Ingredients:

- 1 ripe avocado, peeled and pitted
- 1 (15-ounce) can of chickpeas, rinsed
- 1 medium stalk celery, diced
- ½ large bell pepper, diced
- 1 medium carrot, diced
- 1 lemon, juiced
- ¼ cup cilantro, chopped
- ½ teaspoon salt
- ¼ teaspoon black pepper
- 6 collard leaves

Instructions:

1. Mash the avocado flesh in a suitable bowl, then add chickpeas and crush them with a fork.
2. Stir in celery, bell pepper, carrot, lemon juice, cilantro, black pepper and salt.
3. Mix well and divide this mixture over 6 collard leaves.
4. Roll all the collard leaves into a wrap.
5. Serve.

Serving Suggestion:

Serve these wraps with a quinoa salad.

Storage Tips:

Pack the wraps in a food-grade ziplock bag, and store them in the refrigerator for up to 2 days.

The 30-Minute Gluten-free Vegan Cookbook for Beginners
150 simple, delicious, and nutritious whole food, plant-based, and Gluten-free recipes. Make them in under 30 minutes to improve your health and lose weight

137

Strawberry Chickpea Sandwich

Nutritional Values Per Serving	
Calories	321
Total Fat	8.2g
Saturated Fat	1.2g
Cholesterol	0mg
Sodium	220mq
Total Carbohydrate	50.5g
Dietary Fiber	14.9g
Total Sugars	10.3g
Protein	14.7g

 Servings 2

 Preparation Time 15 minutes

Cooking Time 8 minutes

Ingredients:

- ½ ripe avocado, peeled and pitted
- 1 (15-ounce) can of chickpeas, rinsed
- 1 medium stalk celery, diced
- ½ bell pepper, diced
- 1 medium carrot, diced
- 1 lemon, juiced
- ¾ cup strawberries, diced
- 3 tablespoons plain hummus
- ½ teaspoon salt
- ¼ teaspoon pepper
- Cooking spray
- 4 gluten-free bread slices

Instructions:

1. Mash avocado in a bowl and keep it aside.
2. Add chickpeas to another bowl and mash them with a fork.
3. Stir in celery, carrot, bell pepper, lemon juice, and strawberries to the mashed chickpeas, then mix well.
4. Add mashed avocado, hummus, salt, and black pepper, then mix evenly.
5. Divide the avocado filling over half of the bread slices.
6. Place the other bread slices on top.
7. Grease a skillet with cooking spray and place it over high heat.
8. Sear the sandwiches on both sides for 1-2 minutes until golden brown.
9. Serve.

Storage Tips:

Pack the sandwiches into a sealable container, cover the lid and freeze for no more than 3 months, or refrigerate for no more than 2 days.

Mushroom Avocado Sandwich

Nutritional Values Per Serving	
Calories	310
Total Fat	23.8g
Saturated Fat	4.1g
Cholesterol	0mg
Sodium	420mg
Total Carbohydrate	24.6g
Dietary Fiber	5.8g
Total Sugars	6g
Protein	3.7g

 Servings 4

Preparation Time 20 minutes

 Cooking Time 24 minutes

Ingredients:

Crispy Mushrooms

- 4 white button mushrooms, sliced
- 4 cremini mushrooms, sliced
- 10 shitake mushrooms, sliced
- 2 tablespoons cooking oil
- ⅛ teaspoon garlic powder
- Black pepper, to taste
- Salt, to taste

Sandwich

- 8 gluten-free bread slices
- 16 tomato slices
- 1 large avocado, sliced lengthwise
- 4 leaves of romaine lettuce
- ½ cup garlic aioli
- 4 tablespoons vegan butter

Instructions:

1. Preheat your oven to 400 degrees F.
2. Line a suitable baking sheet with parchment paper and grease it with oil.
3. Spread the mushroom slices on the parchment paper and sprinkle salt, garlic powder and black pepper.
4. Bake the mushroom slices for 10 minutes.
5. Flip the mushrooms and bake for another 10 minutes.
6. Transfer the mushrooms to a plate lined with a paper towel.
7. Brush the gluten-free bread slices with vegan butter and sear them in a skillet until golden brown from both sides.
8. Divide the mushrooms over half of the slices.
9. Add aioli, romaine lettuce, tomato slice, and avocado slice on top of each sandwich filling.
10. Place the other bread slices on top and cut the sandwiches in half.
11. Serve.

Serving Suggestion:

Serve these sandwiches with some baked fries.

Storage Tips:

These sandwiches can be best stored in a freezer, and to do so, pack them in a small ziplock bag or reaction-free container.

The 30-Minute Gluten-free Vegan Cookbook for Beginners
150 simple, delicious, and nutritious whole food, plant-based, and Gluten-free recipes. Make them in under 30 minutes to improve your health and lose weight

139

Pulled Mushroom BBQ Sandwich

 Servings 2

 Preparation Time 15 minutes

 Cooking Time 27 minutes

Nutritional Values Per Serving

Calories	228
Total Fat	5.1g
Saturated Fat	0.8g
Cholesterol	0mg
Sodium	658mg
Total Carbohydrate	43.6g
Dietary Fiber	5.3g
Total Sugars	13.8g
Protein	7.1g

Ingredients:

Gluten-free BBQ Sauce

- 4 cups gluten-free tomato ketchup
- 1 cup light brown sugar
- 8 tablespoons white wine vinegar
- 4 tablespoons gluten-free Worcestershire sauce
- 8 teaspoons smoked Spanish paprika
- 4 teaspoons onion powder
- 4 tablespoons lemon juice

Mushroom Sandwich

- 2 cups gluten-free BBQ sauce
- 22 ounces of shiitake mushrooms
- 22 ounces of baby portobello mushrooms
- 1 tablespoon olive oil
- 1 large white onion, diced
- Salt and black pepper, to taste
- 4 gluten-free bread slices

Toppings

- 2 arugula leaves
- 2 tomato slices
- 2 dill pickle slices

Instructions:

1. Mix ketchup and the rest of the BBQ sauce ingredients in a saucepan.
2. Cook this sauce on medium heat with stirring until it thickens and is reduced to half. Keep it aside to cool.
3. Sauté mushrooms with onions and oil in a large skillet for 7 minutes.
4. Stir in BBQ sauce, salt, and black pepper, and cook to a boil.
5. Reduce the heat and cook for 15 minutes.
6. Divide the mushroom mixture over two bread slices.
7. Add arugula, tomato, and pickle over the mushroom filling.
8. Place the other gluten-free bread slices on top.
9. Serve.

Serving Suggestion:

Serve these sandwiches with vegan coleslaw and oven fries.

Storage Tips:

Pack the sandwiches in a food-grade ziplock bag, flatten this bag and freeze for up to 3 months.

Sweet Potato Sushi Wrap

Nutritional Values Per Serving	
Calories	321
Total Fat	7.8g
Saturated Fat	1.6g
Cholesterol	0mg
Sodium	221mg
Total Carbohydrate	56.2g
Dietary Fiber	7.8g
Total Sugars	9g
Protein	7.2g

 Servings 6

 Preparation Time 20 minutes

 Cooking Time 20 minutes

Ingredients:

Onigirazu

- 4 nori sheets
- 4 cups of cooked sushi rice
- 1 avocado, sliced
- 1-ounce baby spinach
- 1 red cabbage, shredded and pickled
- Sriracha or vegan mayo, to taste

Sweet Potato Version

- 1 large sweet potato, peeled and cut into ½ inch thick sticks
- 1 tablespoon tamari
- 1 tablespoon maple syrup
- 2 teaspoons olive oil
- 1 teaspoon toasted sesame oil
- 2 teaspoons rice vinegar

Instructions:

1. Preheat your oven to 425 degrees F.
2. Line a baking tray with parchment paper.
3. Mix sweet potatoes with tamari, maple syrup, oil, sesame oil, and vinegar in a large mixing bowl.
4. Spread the sweet potatoes over the prepared baking tray.
5. Bake the sweet potatoes for 20 minutes and flip them once cooked halfway through.
6. Spread a nori sheet over a working surface.
7. Add ¼ of the rice on top of the nori sheet and spread it evenly while leaving ½ inch around the edges.
8. Add ¼ sweet potatoes, avocado, spinach, cabbage, and vegan mayo on top of the rice, at the center of nori sheet.
9. Roll the nori sheet into wrap and repeat the same with the remaining steps.
10. Serve.

Serving Suggestion:

Serve with tamari on the side.

Storage Tips:

Do not store these sandwiches in your refrigerator for more than 2 days. For best taste, freeze it in a sealable container for up to 3 months.

The 30-Minute Gluten-free Vegan Cookbook for Beginners
150 simple, delicious, and nutritious whole food, plant-based, and Gluten-free recipes. Make them in under 30 minutes to improve your health and lose weight

141

CHAPTER 08

SPECIAL TREATS AND DESSERTS

Vegan and Gluten Free Recipes Specially for Children

Chocolate-Banana Bites

Nutritional Values Per Serving	
Calories	167
Total Fat	7.6g
Saturated Fat	2.1g
Cholesterol	0mg
Sodium	8mg
Total Carbohydrate	22.5g
Dietary Fiber	2.9g
Total Sugars	13.5g
Protein	4.6g

 Servings 6

 Preparation Time 15 minutes

 Cooking Time 2 minutes

Ingredients:

- 3 large bananas, sliced
- ¼ cup natural peanut butter
- ¾ cup vegan chocolate chips

Instructions:

1. Mix chocolate chips and peanut butter in a microwave-proof bowl.
2. Melt the chocolate in the microwave by heating for 2 minutes on medium heat then mix well.
3. Dip the banana slices into the chocolate and place them on a baking sheet lined with parchment paper.
4. Refrigerate these bites for 10 minutes
5. Serve.

Serving Suggestion:

Drizzle chopped nuts over the banana bites before serving.

Storage Tips:

You can refrigerate or freeze these bites in a sealable container.

The 30-Minute Gluten-free Vegan Cookbook for Beginners
150 simple, delicious, and nutritious whole food, plant-based, and Gluten-free recipes. Make them in under 30 minutes to improve your health and lose weight

Mashed Potatoes

Servings 4

Preparation Time 10 minutes

Cooking Time 20 minutes

Nutritional Values Per Serving

Calories	291
Total Fat	13.5g
Saturated Fat	10.2g
Cholesterol	14mg
Sodium	412mg
Total Carbohydrate	39.9g
Dietary Fiber	5g
Total Sugars	3.3g
Protein	5.7g

Ingredients:

- 4 pounds of red potatoes, peeled and quartered
- 6 garlic cloves, peeled and sliced
- 1 cup almond milk
- ½ cup reduced-fat coconut cream
- 2 tablespoons almond butter, melted
- 2 tablespoons fresh parsley, minced
- 2 tablespoons fresh thyme, minced
- 3 teaspoons fresh rosemary, minced
- 1¼ teaspoons salt

Instructions:

1. Add potatoes and garlic to a Dutch oven and pour in water to cover them.
2. Cook the potatoes for 20 minutes until tender.
3. Drain and mash them in a bowl.
4. Stir in the rest of the ingredients and mix well.
5. Serve.

Serving Suggestion:

Serve these mashed potatoes with glazed carrots.

Storage Tips:

Add the mashed potatoes to a container and refrigerate for 2 days or freeze for up to 3 months.

The 30-Minute Gluten-free Vegan Cookbook for Beginners
150 simple, delicious, and nutritious whole food, plant-based, and Gluten-free recipes. Make them in under 30 minutes to improve your health and lose weight

145

Almond Crispies

 Servings
6

 Preparation Time
10 minutes

 Cooking Time
12 minutes

Nutritional Values Per Serving	
Calories	358
Total Fat	18.2g
Saturated Fat	1.5g
Cholesterol	0mg
Sodium	58mg
Total Carbohydrate	44.7g
Dietary Fiber	3.4g
Total Sugars	19.4g
Protein	5.6g

Ingredients:

- ⅓ cup maple syrup
- ¼ cup canola oil
- 1 tablespoon water
- 1 teaspoon almond extract
- 1 cup brown rice flour
- ½ cup almond flour
- ¼ cup sugar
- 1 teaspoon baking powder
- 1 teaspoon ground cinnamon
- ⅛ teaspoon salt
- ½ cup chopped almonds

Instructions:

1. Mix maple syrup with water, canola oil and almond extract in a bowl.

2. Stir in rice and almond flour, sugar, cinnamon, baking powder, and salt, then mix well until lump-free.

3. Fold in almonds and drop a tablespoonful of the batter onto a baking sheet lined with parchment paper.

4. Preheat your oven to 350 degrees F.

5. Bake the almond crispies for 12 minutes, then allow them to cool.

6. Serve.

Serving Suggestion:

Serve these crispies with a drizzle of melted chocolate on top.

Storage Tips:

Store these crispies at room temperature in a sealed container.

Zucchini Roll-Ups

 Servings
4

 Preparation Time
10 minutes

 Cooking Time
25 minutes

Nutritional Values Per Serving

Calories	151
Total Fat	5.8g
Saturated Fat	3.2g
Cholesterol	20mg
Sodium	576mg
Total Carbohydrate	17g
Dietary Fiber	3.5g
Total Sugars	10g
Protein	10.7g

Ingredients:

- 1 cup vegan ricotta cheese
- 1 ½ teaspoons Italian seasoning
- ¼ teaspoon salt
- ¼ teaspoon black pepper
- 2 medium zucchini
- 4 plum tomatoes, seeded and chopped
- 1 can (8-ounce) tomato sauce
- 1 tablespoon tomato paste
- Shredded vegan Parmesan cheese to garnish

Instructions:

1. Preheat your oven to 425 degrees F.
2. Mix vegan ricotta, ½ teaspoon Italian seasoning, salt, and black pepper in a bowl.
3. Cut the zucchini into 1/8-inch-thick slices.
4. Drop a tablespoon of ricotta cheese mixture on one corner of each zucchini slice and roll them up.
5. Secure the slices with toothpicks and place them on an 8-inch baking dish.
6. Mix tomatoes, tomato paste, tomato sauce, and the remaining 1 teaspoon of Italian seasoning in a bowl.
7. Add this mixture around the roll-ups and bake for 25 minutes.
8. Remove the toothpicks from the rolls.
9. Garnish with Parmesan cheese and serve.

Serving Suggestion:

Enjoy these zucchini rolls with kale chips.

Storage Tips:

Keep these rolls in a sealable container and refrigerate for 2 days or freeze for 2 months.

The 30-Minute Gluten-free Vegan Cookbook for Beginners
150 simple, delicious, and nutritious whole food, plant-based, and Gluten-free recipes. Make them in under 30 minutes to improve your health and lose weight

147

Pineapple Nice Cream

Nutritional Values Per Serving	
Calories	246
Total Fat	0.6g
Saturated Fat	0.2g
Cholesterol	0mg
Sodium	7mg
Total Carbohydrate	62.9g
Dietary Fiber	3.8g
Total Sugars	59.3g
Protein	1.7g

 Servings 2

 Preparation Time 10 minutes

Cooking Time 0 minutes

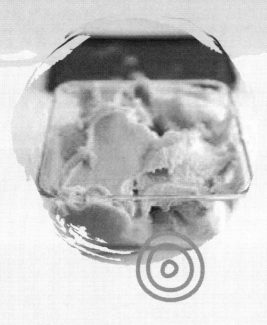

Ingredients:

- 1 (16-ounces) package of frozen pineapple chunks
- 1 cup frozen mango chunks
- 1 tablespoon lemon juice

Instructions:

1. Blend pineapple, mango and lemon juice in a blender until creamy.
2. Add this mixture to a bowl and freeze for 1 hour.
3. Scoop out and serve.

Serving Suggestion:

Serve this nice cream with mango cubes on top.

Storage Tips:

Keep this cream meal packed in a sealed container and refrigerate for up to a month or freeze for 6 months.

Millet Upma

 Servings
4

 Preparation Time
20 minutes

 Cooking Time
27 minutes

Nutritional Values Per Serving	
Calories	141
Total Fat	10.5g
Saturated Fat	1.4g
Cholesterol	0mg
Sodium	27mg
Total Carbohydrate	9.6g
Dietary Fiber	2.7g
Total Sugars	3g
Protein	3.3g

Ingredients:

- ½ cup barnyard millet flakes
- 1¼ cup tap water
- 1 teaspoon split black gram
- 1 cup warm water
- 2 tablespoons olive oil
- ¼ teaspoon mustard seeds
- ¼ teaspoon cumin seeds
- 1 sprig of curry leaves
- 1 green chili, chopped
- 3 tablespoons peanuts, chopped
- 1 onion, chopped
- 1 carrot, chopped
- 3 tablespoons green peas
- 2 pinches of gluten-free asafoetida
- 2 teaspoons of sugar
- ¼ teaspoon turmeric powder
- Salt to taste
- 1 tablespoon fresh coconut, shredded
- 1 tablespoon coriander, chopped
- Juice of 1 lemon

Instructions:

1. Add millet flakes, 1 cup water, and a pinch of salt to a bowl and soak for 1 minute.
2. Drain and squeeze the flakes to remove the water.
3. Soak these flakes again in ¼ cup of salt-free water for 10 minutes
4. Add split black gram to 1 cup of warm water for 10 minutes, then drain.
5. Sauté mustard seeds with oil in a wok for 30 seconds.
6. Add cumin seeds, curry leaves, green chili, and peanuts, then sauté for 1 minute.
7. Add split black gram and sauté for 1 minute.
8. Stir in carrots, onion, and green peas, then cook for 2 minutes.
9. Add asafoetida, salt, turmeric powder, millet flakes, and sugar.
10. Add a splash of water, then cover with a lid and cook for 2 minutes.
11. Stir in lemon juice, coconut, and coriander leaves.
12. Serve.

Serving Suggestion:

Serve this millet upma with roasted carrots.

Storage Tips:

Pack the upma into a container and refrigerate for up to 2 days or freeze for 3 months.

The 30-Minute Gluten-free Vegan Cookbook for Beginners
150 simple, delicious, and nutritious whole food, plant-based, and Gluten-free recipes. Make them in under 30 minutes to improve your health and lose weight

149

Brown Rice Poha

 Servings
6

 Preparation Time
20 minutes

 Cooking Time
17 minutes

Nutritional Values Per Serving

Calories	154
Total Fat	6.4 g
Saturated Fat	0.8 g
Cholesterol	0 mg
Sodium	3 mg
Total Carbohydrate	22.4 g
Dietary Fiber	1.8 g
Total Sugars	7.9 g
Protein	2.4 g

Ingredients:

- 1 cup brown rice flakes
- 4 cups water
- 2 onions, chopped
- 2 green chilies, chopped
- 1 sprig of curry leaves
- 2 tablespoons of peanuts
- 2 tablespoons olive oil
- ¼ teaspoon mustard seeds
- ¼ teaspoon cumin seeds
- ¼ teaspoon turmeric powder
- 1 pinch of gluten-free asafoetida
- 1 tablespoon sugar (optional)
- 1 tablespoon shredded coconut
- 3 tablespoons of pomegranate seeds
- 1 tablespoon of chopped coriander leaves
- 1 tablespoon fresh lemon juice
- Salt to taste

Instructions:

1. Soak rice flakes in 2 cups water mixed with a pinch of salt for 1 minute.
2. Drain and soak again in 2 cups cup of clean water for 10 minutes
3. Drain and keep the flakes aside.
4. Sauté mustard seeds with oil in a wok for 30 seconds.
5. Stir in cumin seeds, curry leaves, green chilies, and peanuts, then cook for 2 minutes.
6. Toss in onions, asafoetida, sugar, and turmeric powder, then sauté for 2 minutes.
7. Add brown rice flakes, cover, and cook for 1 minute.
8. Add lemon juice, coriander leaves, coconut, and pomegranate seeds.
9. Mix well and serve.

Serving Suggestion:

Serve this poha along with zucchini rolls.

Storage Tips:

Place the poha in a sealable container and refrigerate for no more than 3 days or freeze for 3 months. Let it thaw first at room temperature before reheating.

Vegan Parmesan Tomatoes

Nutritional Values Per Serving	
Calories	65
Total Fat	5g
Saturated Fat	0.8g
Cholesterol	0mg
Sodium	157mg
Total Carbohydrate	5g
Dietary Fiber	1.7g
Total Sugars	3.3g
Protein	1.2g

 Servings 4

 Preparation Time 10 minutes

 Cooking Time 15 minutes

Ingredients:

- 4 plum tomatoes, halved
- ¼ cup vegan Parmesan cheese, grated
- 1 teaspoon fresh oregano, chopped
- ¼ teaspoon salt
- 4 teaspoons olive oil
- Black pepper, to taste

Instructions:

1. Preheat your oven to 450 degrees F.
2. Place the halved tomatoes on a suitable baking sheet, with their cut side up.
3. Drizzle olive oil, Parmesan, oregano, salt, and black pepper on top.
4. Bake for 15 minutes in the preheated oven, then serve.

Serving Suggestion:

Enjoy these Parmesan tomatoes with oven fries.

Storage Tips:

Store the tomatoes in a sealed container in your refrigerator for 2 days and reheat in the microwave before serving.

The 30-Minute Gluten-free Vegan Cookbook for Beginners
150 simple, delicious, and nutritious whole food, plant-based, and Gluten-free recipes. Make them in under 30 minutes to improve your health and lose weight

151

Maple Roasted Carrots

Nutritional Values Per Serving	
Calories	78
Total Fat	5.8g
Saturated Fat	3.7g
Cholesterol	15mg
Sodium	335mg
Total Carbohydrate	7g
Dietary Fiber	0.1g
Total Sugars	6.1g
Protein	0.1g

 Servings
4

 Preparation Time
10 minutes

Cooking Time
25 minutes

Ingredients:

- 1½ pounds carrots, peeled and diced
- 2 tablespoons melted almond butter
- 2 tablespoons pure maple syrup
- ½ teaspoon salt
- ¼ teaspoon black pepper
- 2 teaspoons snipped fresh chives

Instructions:

1. Preheat your oven to 400 degrees F.
2. Toss carrots with almond butter, maple syrup, salt, and black pepper in a large bowl.
3. Spread these carrots on a rimmed baking sheet and bake for 25 minutes.
4. Garnish with chives and serve.

Storage Tips:

Pack roasted carrots in a container without chives and refrigerate for up to 3 days or freeze for 3 months.

The 30-Minute Gluten-free Vegan Cookbook for Beginners
150 simple, delicious, and nutritious whole food, plant-based, and Gluten-free recipes. Make them in under 30 minutes to improve your health and lose weight

Fruit Bowl

 Servings
4

 Preparation Time
10 minutes

Cooking Time
0 minutes

Nutritional Values Per Serving

Calories	139
Total Fat	1g
Saturated Fat	0g
Cholesterol	0mg
Sodium	5mg
Total Carbohydrate	34.1g
Dietary Fiber	7.6g
Total Sugars	22.3g
Protein	2.6g

Ingredients:

- 2 cups diced fresh pineapple
- 1 pound strawberries, hulled and sliced
- ½ pint blackberries halved
- 4 ripe kiwis, peeled, halved, and sliced

Instructions:

1. Mix pineapple with strawberries, kiwi, and blackberries in a large bowl.
2. Divide into bowls and serve.

Storage Tips:

Keep the fruit mixture in a sealable container and refrigerate for no more than a day or freeze for 3 months.

The 30-Minute Gluten-free Vegan Cookbook for Beginners
150 simple, delicious, and nutritious whole food, plant-based, and Gluten-free recipes. Make them in under 30 minutes to improve your health and lose weight

153

Vegan Gluten Free Recipes for Pregnant Women

Lamington Bliss Balls

 Servings
8

 Preparation Time
15 minutes

 Cooking Time
3 minutes

Nutritional Values Per Serving

Calories	298
Total Fat	25.3g
Saturated Fat	16.6g
Cholesterol	0mg
Sodium	11mg
Total Carbohydrate	19g
Dietary Fiber	4.6g
Total Sugars	8.5g
Protein	4.5g

Ingredients:

- 1 cup raw cashews
- ⅓ cup desiccated coconut
- ¼ cup maple syrup
- 2 tablespoons coconut oil
- ½ cup whole raspberries

Chocolate layer

- ⅓ cup cocoa powder
- ¼ cup maple syrup
- 4 tablespoons coconut oil
- 2 tablespoons coconut cream
- ½ cup desiccated coconut

Instructions:

1. Add coconut and cashews to a food processor and blend until crumbly.
2. Pour in coconut oil and maple syrup, then blend again to mix evenly.
3. Take 2 tablespoons of this cashew mixture and wrap it around a raspberry.
4. Roll the mixture into a ball and make more in the same way.
5. Place these bliss balls on a tray lined with parchment paper.
6. Now mix cocoa powder, maple, coconut oil, and coconut cream in a saucepan.
7. Mix and cook this mixture at medium-high heat for 3 minutes.
8. Allow this mixture to cool, then dip the balls in the cocoa cream.
9. Coat the chocolate-coated balls with desiccated coconut.
10. Return the balls to the tray and refrigerate them for 30 minutes.
11. Serve.

Storage Tips:

Store balls in an airtight container in the refrigerator for up to 3 days, or you can store them in your freezer for up to 1 month.

The 30-Minute Gluten-free Vegan Cookbook for Beginners
150 simple, delicious, and nutritious whole food, plant-based, and Gluten-free recipes. Make them in under 30 minutes to improve your health and lose weight

155

Quinoa with Peas

Nutritional Values Per Serving	
Calories	301
Total Fat	9.8g
Saturated Fat	1.9g
Cholesterol	0mg
Sodium	353mq
Total Carbohydrate	35.4g
Dietary Fiber	6.4g
Total Sugars	2.1g
Protein	17.3g

 Servings 2

 Preparation Time 10 minutes

Cooking Time 30 minutes

Ingredients:

- 1 carrot, chopped
- ½ onion, chopped
- Salt, to taste
- 2 cups water
- 1 cup quinoa
- ½ cup peas, boiled
- 2 tablespoons olive oil

Instructions:

1. Add the rinsed quinoa with 2 cups water to a cooking pot and cook for 20 minutes until tender.
2. Drain and keep the quinoa aside.
3. Sauté onion and carrot in olive oil in a large pot for 5 minutes.
4. Stir in peas, salt, and quinoa, then cook for 5 minutes.
5. Serve.

Serving Suggestion:

Serve the quinoa with garlicky roasted eggplant.

Storage Tips:

Store the quinoa in a sealable container for up to 3 days or freeze for up to 3 months.

Chocolate and Peanut Butter Bark

Nutritional Values Per Serving	
Calories	190
Total Fat	10.6g
Saturated Fat	2.6g
Cholesterol	0mg
Sodium	256mg
Total Carbohydrate	14.4g
Dietary Fiber	1.4g
Total Sugars	6.7g
Protein	11.2g

 Servings 6

 Preparation Time 15 minutes

 Cooking Time 0 minutes

Ingredients:

- 4 ounces vegan dark chocolate
- ¼ cup peanut butter
- 3 tablespoons chopped peanuts
- ¼ teaspoon sea salt

Instructions:

1. Add dark chocolate to a bowl and melt it by heating it in the microwave on Low power.
2. Stir in peanut butter and peanuts.
3. Line a baking sheet with parchment paper.
4. Spread the chocolate mixture on the baking sheet and sprinkle salt on top.
5. Refrigerate this chocolate bark for 30 minutes, then break it into pieces.
6. Serve.

Storage Tips:

Store the bark in a cookie jar in the refrigerator for up to 15 days or place it in your freezer for 6 months.

The 30-Minute Gluten-free Vegan Cookbook for Beginners
150 simple, delicious, and nutritious whole food, plant-based, and Gluten-free recipes. Make them in under 30 minutes to improve your health and lose weight

157

Quinoa Black Bean Salad

Nutritional Values Per Serving

Calories	297
Total Fat	18.3g
Saturated Fat	2.6g
Cholesterol	0mg
Sodium	37mg
Total Carbohydrate	29.6g
Dietary Fiber	6.4g
Total Sugars	3.6g
Protein	7.4g

 Servings 6

 Preparation Time 10 minutes

 Cooking Time 1 minute

Ingredients:

- ½ cup quinoa
- 1 cup water
- 1 ½ cups boiled black beans
- 1 cup of fresh corn
- 1 cup bell peppers
- 1 cup chopped tomatoes
- ½ cup onion, chopped
- 1 cup chopped cucumber
- 2 tablespoons cilantro

Dressing

- 2 tablespoon lime juice
- ½ cup light olive oil
- Salt to taste
- ½ teaspoon black pepper powder

Instructions:

1. Add quinoa along with 1 cup of water to the Instant Pot and seal the lid.
2. Cook on Manual mode with High pressure for 1 minute.
3. Once done, leave the Instant Pot to release the pressure naturally in 10 minutes, then remove the lid.
4. Mix lime juice, oil, salt, and black pepper in a bowl.
5. Add cooked quinoa, corn, bell peppers, tomatoes, onion, cucumber, cilantro, and black beans to a mixing bowl.
6. Stir in the lime dressing and mix well.
7. Serve.

Serving Suggestion:

Serve this salad with corn tortilla chips.

Storage Tips:

Keep the salad in a sealable container and refrigerate for no more than 24 hours. Freezing is not recommended.

Zucchini with Basil Pesto

 Servings
2

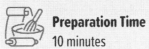 **Preparation Time**
10 minutes

 Cooking Time
5 minutes

Nutritional Values Per Serving	
Calories	150
Total Fat	10.6g
Saturated Fat	0.9g
Cholesterol	0mg
Sodium	33mg
Total Carbohydrate	12.7g
Dietary Fiber	4.1g
Total Sugars	6.1g
Protein	5.9g

Ingredients:

- 2 large zucchini
- A dash of olive oil
- 2 tablespoons basil pesto
- A handful of pine nuts

Instructions:

1. Pass both zucchini through a spiralizer to make long zucchini curls.
2. Sauté zucchini with oil in a frying pan for 3 minutes.
3. Stir in pesto and pine nuts, then cook for 2 minutes.
4. Serve.

Storage Tips:

Store the zucchini in a sealable container, then refrigerator for 2 days or freeze for 3 months.

The 30-Minute Gluten-free Vegan Cookbook for Beginners
150 simple, delicious, and nutritious whole food, plant-based, and Gluten-free recipes. Make them in under 30 minutes to improve your health and lose weight

159

Sweet Potato Flapjacks

 Servings
4

 Preparation Time
15 minutes

 Cooking Time
25 minutes

Nutritional Values Per Serving

Calories	226
Total Fat	12.5g
Saturated Fat	1.6g
Cholesterol	0mg
Sodium	72mg
Total Carbohydrate	25.2g
Dietary Fiber	4.4g
Total Sugars	2.9g
Protein	5.5g

Ingredients:

- 1 sweet potato, grated
- 3 teaspoons pea protein
- 6 teaspoons of sunflower oil
- ½ ounce pumpkin seeds
- 1 ounce chopped sun-dried tomatoes
- 7 ounces rolled oats
- 1½ ounce cocoa butter
- 3 teaspoons vegan bouillon
- 2 teaspoons tomato puree
- 1 teaspoon dried oregano

Instructions:

1. Preheat your oven to 390 degrees F.
2. Add cocoa butter to a large bowl and melt in the microwave.
3. Stir in sweet potato, oats, sun-dried tomatoes, tomato puree, pea protein, and sunflower oil.
4. Add pumpkin seeds, oregano, and bouillon to the bowl then mix well to coat.
5. Drop circles of this sweet potato mixture onto a baking sheet and bake for 25 minutes.
6. Serve warm.

Storage Tips:

Keep the flapjacks in a sealable container and refrigerate for no more than 3 days or freeze for 3 months.

Chocolate Swirl Mousse

Nutritional Values Per Serving

Calories	362
Total Fat	7.9g
Saturated Fat	6.4g
Cholesterol	0mg
Sodium	23mg
Total Carbohydrate	70.7g
Dietary Fiber	8.3g
Total Sugars	44g
Protein	5.1g

 Servings
1

 Preparation Time
10 minutes

 Cooking Time
0 minutes

Ingredients:

- 1 ripe banana, mashed
- 1 tablespoon coconut flour
- 1 tablespoon raw cacao powder
- 1 tablespoon pure maple syrup
- ¼ teaspoon pure vanilla extract
- 2 tablespoons coconut cream

Instructions:

1. Mix mashed banana with coconut flour, cacao powder, maple syrup, and vanilla extract in a bowl.
2. Stir in coconut cream and stir gently to make a swirl effect.
3. Refrigerate for 15-20 minutes, then serve.

Serving Suggestion:

Sprinkle roasted seeds and nuts over the mousse before serving.

Storage Tips:

Store the mousse in a bowl, cover, and refrigerate for up to 2 days.

The 30-Minute Gluten-free Vegan Cookbook for Beginners
150 simple, delicious, and nutritious whole food, plant-based, and Gluten-free recipes. Make them in under 30 minutes to improve your health and lose weight

161

Sweet Potato Black Bean Patties

Nutritional Values Per Serving

Calories	335
Total Fat	3g
Saturated Fat	0.4g
Cholesterol	0mg
Sodium	83mg
Total Carbohydrate	67.3g
Dietary Fiber	13g
Total Sugars	2.1g
Protein	11.9g

 Servings 4

 Preparation Time 20 minutes

Cooking Time 30 minutes

Ingredients:

- 2 cans of black beans
- 2 medium sweet potatoes, diced
- 1 cup crushed corn tortilla chips
- ½ red onion, diced
- ½ cup coriander, diced
- ½ cup sweet corn

- 1 tablespoon paprika
- 1 teaspoon garlic powder
- 1 teaspoon cumin
- Pinch of chili powder
- ½ cup of polenta flour to coat
- Salt to taste

Instructions:

1. Preheat your oven to 400 degrees F.
2. Add sweet potatoes to a pot filled with water and boil them for 10 minutes
3. Drain and add the sweet potatoes to a bowl, then mash them with a fork.
4. Stir in black beans, onion, coriander, and the rest of the ingredients except polenta flour.
5. Make 4 patties out of this mixture and coat them with polenta flour.
6. Place patties on a baking tray lined with parchment paper.
7. Bake the patties for 20 minutes and flip them once cooked halfway through.
8. Serve.

Serving Suggestion:

Serve the patties with gluten-free bread and vegan coleslaw.

Storage Tips:

Keep the uncooked patties in a sealable bag and freeze and cook before serving.

Socca Tacos and Peach Salsa

Nutritional Values Per Serving

Calories	404
Total Fat	15.2g
Saturated Fat	2.6g
Cholesterol	0mg
Sodium	46mg
Total Carbohydrate	55.5g
Dietary Fiber	13.4g
Total Sugars	24.3g
Protein	15.3g

 Servings
4

 Preparation Time
20 minutes

 Cooking Time
19 minutes

Ingredients:

Hot filling

- 1 chipotle chili, chopped
- 1 teaspoon olive oil
- 1 red onion, chopped
- 4 garlic cloves, chopped
- 1 (14-ounce) can pinto beans, rinsed and drained
- 1 medium tomato, chopped
- 1 teaspoon ground cumin
- 1 teaspoon smoked paprika
- 2 teaspoons tamari

Peach salsa

- 1 avocado, pitted and diced
- 4 Saturn peaches, pitted and diced
- 2 medium tomatoes, chopped
- Juice of 1 lime
- 1 handful of coriander stems, chopped
- 4 romaine lettuce leaves, cut into ribbons

Socca

- 7 ounces chickpea flour
- 1 ¼ cup of water
- Olive oil for cooking

Instructions:

1. Mix chickpea flour with water in a bowl until there are no lumps.
2. Keep this chickpea batter aside for a while.
3. Add chipotle chili to a bowl filled with boiling water for 2-3 minutes.
4. Mix all the peach salsa ingredients in a bowl.
5. Remove the soaked chilies from the water and chop them.
6. Sauté onion, garlic, and tomato with oil in a frying pan for 5 minutes.
7. Stir in paprika, chili, tamari, cumin, and pinto beans, cook for 5 minutes, then transfer to a bowl.
8. Set a suitable non-stick frying pan over medium heat and grease it with oil.
9. Pour 1/6 of the chickpea batter into the pan and cook for 2-3 minutes per side.
10. Make more tortillas in the same way.
11. Place a tortilla on a working surface and add 1/6 of the bean filling.
12. Roll the tortilla into a burrito and make more in the same way.
13. Serve the tacos for salsa.

Storage Tips:

Wrap the tacos in food-grade paper and refrigerate for up to 2 days and reheat before serving. Alternatively, you can store filling, salsa, and tortillas separately in the refrigerator and assemble them before serving.

The 30-Minute Gluten-free Vegan Cookbook for Beginners
150 simple, delicious, and nutritious whole food, plant-based, and Gluten-free recipes. Make them in under 30 minutes to improve your health and lose weight

163

Glowing Pregnancy Smoothie

Nutritional Values Per Serving	
Calories	222
Total Fat	17.3g
Saturated Fat	13.1g
Cholesterol	0mg
Sodium	148mg
Total Carbohydrate	14.6g
Dietary Fiber	8.4g
Total Sugars	3.2g
Protein	8g

 Servings 2

 Preparation Time 5 minutes

 Cooking Time 0 minutes

Ingredients:

- 1 large handful of fresh spinach
- 1 small cucumber, peeled and sliced
- ¼ cup fresh mint leaves
- 2" knob of fresh ginger peeled and chopped
- 1 ½ tablespoons chia seeds
- 1 scoop Raspberry Lemonade Magnesium Powder
- 2 scoops of collagen peptides
- 1 ½ cups mango cubes
- ¾ cup coconut water
- ½ cup almond milk
- 1 handful of ice cubes

Instructions:

1. Blend spinach with the rest of the smoothie ingredients in a high-speed blender for 2 minutes.
2. Serve chilled.

Storage Tips:

Keep the smoothie in a sealable bottle and seal it to refrigerate for no more than 2 days.

Vegan Convalescents

Lemon Apple Ginger Shot

Nutritional Values Per Serving	
Calories	122
Total Fat	0.5g
Saturated Fat	0.3g
Cholesterol	0mg
Sodium	19mg
Total Carbohydrate	31g
Dietary Fiber	5.7g
Total Sugars	23.5g
Protein	0.5g

  Servings
1

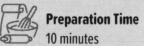 **Preparation Time**
10 minutes

 Cooking Time
0 minutes

Ingredients:

- 1 apple, cored and diced
- ½ lemon juice
- ½ ounce ginger
- 1 teaspoon ground turmeric
- 1 cup water
- 1 tablespoon date syrup

Instructions:

1. Blend apple with lemon juice, ginger, turmeric, water, and date syrup in a blender for 1 minute.
2. Refrigerate this shot for 30 minutes.
3. Serve.

Storage Tips:

Fill into a glass bottle and keep refrigerated for up to one week.

Blueberry Cashew Milk

Nutritional Values Per Serving	
Calories	122
Total Fat	0.5 g
Saturated Fat	0.3 g
Cholesterol	0 mg
Sodium	19 mg
Total Carbohydrate	31 g
Dietary Fiber	5.7 g
Total Sugars	23.5 g
Protein	0.5 g

 Servings
4

 Preparation Time
10 minutes

 Cooking Time
3 minutes

Ingredients:

- 1 cup cashews
- 5 cups filtered water
- 1 pinch of sea salt
- 1 tablespoon baobab powder
- ¾ cup frozen blueberries
- 1 teaspoon vanilla extract
- 1 tablespoon agave syrup

Instructions:

1. Soak cashews in 2 cups of water in a bowl for 6 hours.
2. Drain and rinse the cashews, then transfer them to a blender.
3. Add remaining water and salt, then blend for 3 minutes until smooth.
4. Add baobab powder, blueberries, vanilla, and agave to the blender.
5. Blend again until smooth, then serve.

Serving Suggestion:

Garnish with blueberries and a pinch of baobab powder.

Storage Tips:

Fill into a glass bottle and keep refrigerated for up to one week.

The 30-Minute Gluten-free Vegan Cookbook for Beginners
150 simple, delicious, and nutritious whole food, plant-based, and Gluten-free recipes. Make them in under 30 minutes to improve your health and lose weight

167

Vegan Laksa

Nutritional Values Per Serving

Calories	364
Total Fat	13.6g
Saturated Fat	9.1g
Cholesterol	0mg
Sodium	54mq
Total Carbohydrate	59.5g
Dietary Fiber	8.9g
Total Sugars	11.1g
Protein	10.8g

 Servings 6

 Preparation Time 15 minutes

Cooking Time 20 minutes

Ingredients:

- 4 spring onions, chopped
- 4 garlic cloves
- 1 red chili, deseeded and chopped
- 1 teaspoon ginger, chopped
- 1 teaspoon ground turmeric
- 1 teaspoon olive oil

- 4 cups vegetable stock
- 1 (15-ounce) can of coconut milk
- 3 ½ ounces bean sprouts
- 10 baby corn, halved
- 3 ½ ounces mangetout beans

Serve

- 5 ounces rice noodles
- 1 lime
- Handful cilantro/coriander

Instructions:

1. Blend spring onions with turmeric, garlic, ginger, and chili in a blender until smooth.
2. Sauté this spice paste with olive oil in a large pot for 3 minutes.
3. Stir in vegetable stock and coconut milk, then cook to a boil.
4. Reduce the heat, then add bean sprouts, mangetout beans, and baby corn. Cook for 5 minutes.
5. Meanwhile, cook rice noodles as per the package's instructions, then drain.
6. Divide the rice noodles into serving bowls.
7. Pour the soup over the rice noodles and garnish with coriander and lime juice.
8. Serve warm.

Serving Suggestion:

Serve the laksa with your favorite salad.

Storage Tips:

Store the laksa in a sealable container, then freeze for up to 3 months.

Orange Banana Smoothie

Nutritional Values Per Serving	
Calories	244
Total Fat	0.7g
Saturated Fat	0.2g
Cholesterol	0mg
Sodium	3mg
Total Carbohydrate	62g
Dietary Fiber	7.5g
Total Sugars	43.5g
Protein	3g

 Servings
1

 Preparation Time
5 minutes

 Cooking Time
0 minutes

Ingredients:

- 1 orange, peeled and segmented
- 1 banana, sliced
- 1 cup almond milk
- 1 tablespoon maple syrup
- 4 ice cubes

Instructions:

1. Blend orange segments with banana, milk, maple syrup, and ice cubes in a blender until smooth.
2. Serve.

Storage Tips:

Store the smoothie in a sealed bottle for up to 2-3 days.

The 30-Minute Gluten-free Vegan Cookbook for Beginners
150 simple, delicious, and nutritious whole food, plant-based, and Gluten-free recipes. Make them in under 30 minutes to improve your health and lose weight

169

Zucchini Soup with Basil

 Servings
2

 Preparation Time
10 minutes

Cooking Time
13 minutes

Nutritional Values Per Serving

Calories	172
Total Fat	9.2g
Saturated Fat	2.4g
Cholesterol	0mg
Sodium	504mg
Total Carbohydrate	24g
Dietary Fiber	6.8g
Total Sugars	12.4g
Protein	6.9g

Ingredients:

- 1 tablespoon olive oil
- 1 onion chopped
- 2 ¼ lbs. zucchini, chopped
- 1 garlic clove, chopped
- 1 ¼ pint vegetable stock
- 1 handful of basil leaves, chopped
- ¼ teaspoon salt and black pepper

Serve

- 1 spiralized zucchini
- 1 sprinkle black pepper

Instructions:

1. Sauté onion with olive oil in a large pot for 3 minutes until soft.
2. Stir in garlic and zucchini, then cover and reduce the heat to low.
3. Cook for 7 minutes, then add basil and vegetable stock and cook for 5 minutes.
4. Adjust seasoning with black pepper and salt.
5. Puree this soup in a blender until smooth.
6. Garnish with spiralized zucchini and black pepper.
7. Enjoy hot.

Serving Suggestion:

Serve this soup with a bowl of white rice on the side.

Storage Tips:

Transfer the soup to a food-grade plastic bag, flatten this bag and refrigerate for no more than 2 days or you can freeze it for up to 3 months.

Pea Soup

 Servings
2

 Preparation Time
10 minutes

Cooking Time
15 minutes

Nutritional Values Per Serving

Calories	191
Total Fat	10.2g
Saturated Fat	3.9g
Cholesterol	0mg
Sodium	1169mg
Total Carbohydrate	25.3g
Dietary Fiber	7.8g
Total Sugars	10.9g
Protein	6.8g

Ingredients:

- 1 tablespoon olive oil
- 1 onion, chopped
- 3 cups vegetable stock
- 3 cups frozen peas
- Herbs to garnish
- Olive oil, to garnish

Instructions:

1. Sauté onion with oil in a large saucepan for 5 minutes.
2. Pour in the vegetable stock and cook for 5 minutes.
3. Stir in peas, then cook for 5 minutes on a simmer.
4. Puree this soup with a hand blender until smooth.
5. Garnish with your favorite herbs and olive oil.
6. Serve.

Storage Tips:

Keep the soup in a sealable container and refrigerate for no more than 2 days or freeze it for about 3 months.

The 30-Minute Gluten-free Vegan Cookbook for Beginners
150 simple, delicious, and nutritious whole food, plant-based, and Gluten-free recipes. Make them in under 30 minutes to improve your health and lose weight

171

Beetroot Soup

Nutritional Values Per Serving

Calories	133
Total Fat	9.3g
Saturated Fat	3.2g
Cholesterol	0mg
Sodium	851mg
Total Carbohydrate	16.4g
Dietary Fiber	2.7g
Total Sugars	12g
Protein	2g

 Servings 4

 Preparation Time 10 minutes

Cooking Time 30 minutes

Ingredients:

- 17 ounces raw beets, diced into chunks
- 2 tablespoons olive oil
- 1 red onion chopped
- 1 stick of celery, chopped
- 4 ¼ cups vegetable stock
- 2 tablespoons dill, chopped
- Salt and black pepper to taste

Instructions:

1. Preheat your oven to 450 degrees F.
2. Place the diced beetroots on a baking tray and drizzle 1 tbsp. olive oil over them.
3. Roast the beetroots for 20 minutes.
4. Sauté onion with celery and 1 tbsp. olive oil in a large soup pot for 5 minutes.
5. Stir in roasted beets, vegetable stock, salt, dill, and black pepper, then bring to a boil.
6. Puree the soup until smooth.
7. Serve warm.

Serving Suggestion:

Enjoy this soup with roasted asparagus sticks.

Storage Tips:

Pack the soup in a small ziplock bag or reaction-free container and refrigerate for no more than 3 days or you can freeze it for 3 months.

The 30-Minute Gluten-free Vegan Cookbook for Beginners
150 simple, delicious, and nutritious whole food, plant-based, and Gluten-free recipes. Make them in under 30 minutes to improve your health and lose weight

Turmeric Tonic

Nutritional Values Per Serving

Calories	257
Total Fat	19g
Saturated Fat	1.5g
Cholesterol	0mg
Sodium	120mg
Total Carbohydrate	17g
Dietary Fiber	5.3g
Total Sugars	7.8g
Protein	8.2g

 Servings 4

 Preparation Time 22 minutes

 Cooking Time 0 minutes

Ingredients:

- 1 cup (4 ounces) mixed raw almonds and cashews
- 4 teaspoons grated fresh turmeric
- 2 teaspoons grated fresh ginger
- 2 tablespoons maple syrup
- 1 teaspoon vanilla extract
- 4 cups of filtered water
- ¼ teaspoon sea salt
- 1 pinch of black pepper

Instructions:

1. Add nuts to a medium bowl and pour in enough water to cover them. Soak for 12 hours.
2. Drain and blend the nuts with the remaining water and the rest of the ingredients until smooth.
3. Strain the tonic through a cheesecloth.
4. Serve.

Serving Suggestion:

Sprinkle cinnamon powder over the tonic and serve.

Storage Tips:

Keep the tonic in a sealable glass container and refrigerate for no more than 7 days.

The 30-Minute Gluten-free Vegan Cookbook for Beginners
150 simple, delicious, and nutritious whole food, plant-based, and Gluten-free recipes. Make them in under 30 minutes to improve your health and lose weight

173

Mint Tea

Nutritional Values Per Serving	
Calories	87
Total Fat	1.4g
Saturated Fat	0.3g
Cholesterol	0mg
Sodium	44mg
Total Carbohydrate	16.9g
Dietary Fiber	10g
Total Sugars	2.2g
Protein	4.6g

 Servings 2

 Preparation Time 10 minutes

 Cooking Time 5 minutes

Ingredients:

- 20 fresh mint leaves
- 2 cups water
- 1 teaspoon sugar
- 2 lemon slices to serve
- 6 cardamom pods, crushed
- 1 teaspoon fennel seeds
- 3 springs of fresh thyme
- 2 sprigs of fresh rosemary

Instructions:

1. Crush the mint leaves with a muddler.
2. Add water, mint leaves, and the rest of the ingredients to a cooking pot.
3. Boil this mint tea gently for 5 minutes.
4. Strain and serve.

Serving Suggestion:

Garnish with mint leaves and lemon slices.

Storage Tips:

Store the tea in a bottle and refrigerate for up to 7 days.

Ginger Tea

 Servings
8

 Preparation Time
10 minutes

Cooking Time
25 minutes

Nutritional Values Per Serving

Calories	151
Total Fat	0.3g
Saturated Fat	0.1g
Cholesterol	0mg
Sodium	11mg
Total Carbohydrate	39.5g
Dietary Fiber	0.8g
Total Sugars	35.6g
Protein	0.6g

Ingredients:

- 8 ounces ginger root, chopped
- 2 lemons, juiced
- 8 cups water
- ⅛ cup maple syrup

Instructions:

1. Add ginger root, lemon juice, water, and maple syrup to a cooking pot.
2. Cook this tea on a simmer for 25 minutes.
3. Strain and serve.

Serving Suggestion:

Garnish with a lemon slice.

Storage Tips:

Store the tea in a bottle and refrigerate for up to 7 days.

The 30-Minute Gluten-free Vegan Cookbook for Beginners
150 simple, delicious, and nutritious whole food, plant-based, and Gluten-free recipes. Make them in under 30 minutes to improve your health and lose weight

175

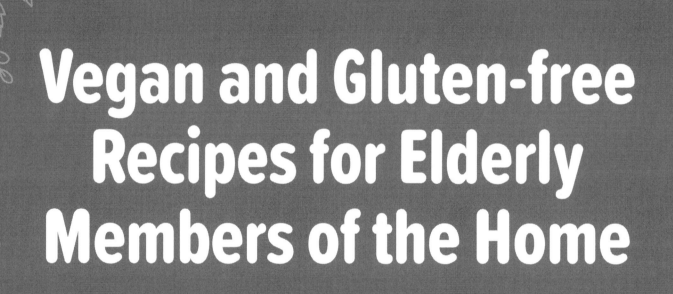

Vegan and Gluten-free Recipes for Elderly Members of the Home

Carrot-Ginger Juice

 Servings
2

 Preparation Time
10 minutes

 Cooking Time
0 minutes

Nutritional Values Per Serving

Calories	190
Total Fat	0.1g
Saturated Fat	0g
Cholesterol	0mg
Sodium	147mg
Total Carbohydrate	47g
Dietary Fiber	8.6g
Total Sugars	31.3g
Protein	5.2g

Ingredients:

- 5 large carrots
- 1 romaine heart
- 2 clementines, peeled
- ½ lemon, peeled
- 1-inch knob of fresh ginger

Instructions:

1. Run the carrots through a juicer, then run the rest of the ingredients to juice them.
2. Stir the extracted juice together and serve.

Storage Tips:

Pour into a glass bottle and keep it refrigerated for up to one week.

The 30-Minute Gluten-free Vegan Cookbook for Beginners
150 simple, delicious, and nutritious whole food, plant-based, and Gluten-free recipes. Make them in under 30 minutes to improve your health and lose weight

177

Beet Apple Juice

Nutritional Values Per Serving

Calories	208
Total Fat	4.7g
Saturated Fat	0.5g
Cholesterol	0mg
Sodium	143mg
Total Carbohydrate	40.3g
Dietary Fiber	11.8g
Total Sugars	24.1g
Protein	5.1g

 Servings 2

 Preparation Time 10 minutes

 Cooking Time 5 minutes

Ingredients:

- 2 medium beets, trimmed and scrubbed
- 1 Granny Smith apple, peeled and cored
- 3 medium carrots, peeled
- 1 tablespoon chia seeds

Instructions:

1. Run the carrots, apples, and beets through a juicer.
2. Stir the extracted juice together.
3. Now add chia seeds to the juice and let them soak for 5 minutes.
4. Mix again and serve.

Serving Suggestion:

Garnish with a slice of apple or beet before serving.

Storage Tips:

Pour into a glass bottle and keep it refrigerated for up to one week.

Garlicky Roasted Eggplant

Nutritional Values Per Serving	
Calories	355
Total Fat	27.7g
Saturated Fat	5.3g
Cholesterol	0mg
Sodium	67mg
Total Carbohydrate	24.5g
Dietary Fiber	8.3g
Total Sugars	16.1g
Protein	5.1g

 Servings
2

 Preparation Time
15 minutes

 Cooking Time
30 minutes

Ingredients:

- 1 eggplant, cut into ½-inch slices
- 2 cloves garlic, chopped
- ¼ cup olive oil
- 1 teaspoon Mediterranean spice blend
- 1 cup coconut yogurt
- 1 clove garlic, chopped
- 1 tablespoon lemon juice
- 1 teaspoon maple syrup

Instructions:

1. Preheat your oven to 400 degrees F.
2. Season the eggplant slices with 2 cloves chopped garlic, oil, and spice blend.
3. Place these eggplant slices on a baking sheet and roast for 30 minutes.
4. Flip them once cooked halfway through.
5. Mix coconut yogurt with 1 clove chopped garlic, lemon juice, and maple syrup in a bowl.
6. Serve the eggplant slices with yogurt sauce.
7. Enjoy.

Storage Tips:

Keep the slices stored in a sealable container and refrigerate for up to 2 days or freeze for up to 3 months. Store the yogurt separately.

The 30-Minute Gluten-free Vegan Cookbook for Beginners
150 simple, delicious, and nutritious whole food, plant-based, and Gluten-free recipes. Make them in under 30 minutes to improve your health and lose weight

179

Coconut Chickpea Curry

Nutritional Values Per Serving	
Calories	336
Total Fat	8.8g
Saturated Fat	6.1g
Cholesterol	0mg
Sodium	1863mg
Total Carbohydrate	54.9g
Dietary Fiber	17.9g
Total Sugars	14.9g
Protein	13g

 Servings 2

 Preparation Time 20 minutes

 Cooking Time 29 minutes

Ingredients:

- 1 tablespoon coconut oil
- 1 large onion, diced
- 4 garlic cloves, minced
- 1 medium knob of fresh ginger, grated
- 1 teaspoon salt
- ½ teaspoon black pepper
- 1 ½ tablespoon curry powder
- 1 (14 ½-ounce) can coconut milk
- 1 (14 ½-ounce) can crushed tomatoes
- 1 (14 ½-ounce) can chickpeas, rinsed
- 2 fresh limes, juices
- Fresh cilantro, chopped, to garnish

Instructions:

1. Sauté onion with oil in a large skillet for 8 minutes.
2. Stir in ginger and garlic, then cook for 1 minute.
3. Add black pepper, salt, curry powder, coconut milk, and tomatoes.
4. Mix well and cook for 15 minutes.
5. Stir in chickpeas and cook for 5 minutes.
6. Add lime juice and cilantro.
7. Serve warm.

Serving Suggestion:

Enjoy the curry with a bowl of white rice on the side.

Storage Tips:

Transfer the curry to a sealable container or a food-grade ziplock bag, seal it, and refrigerate it for no more than 2 days or freeze it for up to 3 months.

Mushroom and Leek Risotto

 Servings
2

 Preparation Time
15 minutes

 Cooking Time
30 minutes

Nutritional Values Per Serving	
Calories	396
Total Fat	23g
Saturated Fat	3.3g
Cholesterol	0mg
Sodium	1545mg
Total Carbohydrate	32.1g
Dietary Fiber	3.8g
Total Sugars	5.1g
Protein	19.3g

Ingredients:

- 4 cups vegetable broth
- 2 tablespoons olive oil
- 8 ounces Bella mushrooms, sliced
- Salt and black pepper to taste
- ¾ cup sliced leeks
- 1 cup arborio rice
- ¼ cup dry white wine
- 1 tablespoon vegan butter
- ¼ cup vegan Parmesan cheese
- Fresh chopped parsley to garnish

Instructions:

1. Sauté mushrooms with 1 tablespoon oil in a cooking pot for 5 minutes, then transfer to a bowl.
2. Add 1 tablespoon oil, salt, black pepper, and leeks to the same pot.
3. Sauté for 3 minutes, then add rice and wine.
4. Cook until the wine is absorbed, then pour in vegetable broth.
5. Reduce the heat to a simmer, then cook until the liquid is absorbed.
6. Add vegan butter, sauteed mushrooms, and vegan Parmesan cheese, cover, and leave the risotto for 5 minutes.
7. Garnish with parsley and serve warm.

Serving Suggestion:

Serve this risotto with a bowl of chickpea salad on the side.

Storage Tips:

Transfer the risotto to a food-grade plastic bag, flatten this bag and refrigerate for no more than 2 days or you can freeze it for up to 3 months.

The 30-Minute Gluten-free Vegan Cookbook for Beginners
150 simple, delicious, and nutritious whole food, plant-based, and Gluten-free recipes. Make them in under 30 minutes to improve your health and lose weight

181

Stuffed Green Peppers

Nutritional Values Per Serving	
Calories	314
Total Fat	5.5g
Saturated Fat	1.1g
Cholesterol	0mg
Sodium	501mg
Total Carbohydrate	54.2g
Dietary Fiber	4.9g
Total Sugars	11.3g
Protein	15.2g

Servings
4

 Preparation Time
20 minutes

 Cooking Time
30 minutes

Ingredients:

- 4 green bell peppers, large
- 1 pound tofu, crumbled
- 1 cup rice, uncooked
- ½ cup onion, peeled and chopped
- 1 ½ cups tomato sauce, unsalted
- Black pepper, to taste

Instructions:

1. Cut the top of the green peppers and remove their seeds and core.
2. Place the bell peppers in boiling water for 5 minutes, then remove them with tongs.
3. Preheat your oven to 400 degrees F.
4. Sauté tofu with rice, onion, tomato sauce, and black pepper for 5 minutes.
5. Place the prepared peppers in a baking dish cut side up.
6. Divide the tofu filling inside the peppers.
7. Bake the stuffed peppers for 20 minutes.
8. Serve warm.

Storage Tips:

Keep the peppers in a sealable container and refrigerate for no more than 2 days or freeze them for up to 3 months. Alternatively, store the filling separately in a separate container and assemble the peppers before cooking.

Mashed Potato Cakes

 Servings 4

 Preparation Time 20 minutes

 Cooking Time 15 minutes

Nutritional Values Per Serving

Calories	386
Total Fat	24.8g
Saturated Fat	4.2g
Cholesterol	2mg
Sodium	1002mg
Total Carbohydrate	32.9g
Dietary Fiber	4.8g
Total Sugars	2g
Protein	10.4g

Ingredients:

- 2 cups cold mashed potatoes
- 1 cup vegan shredded cheese
- ½ cup almond flour
- 1 tablespoon olive oil
- 1 medium onion chopped
- 2 cloves garlic chopped
- 1 teaspoon salt
- ½ teaspoon black pepper
- 2 tablespoons fresh basil chopped
- 2 tablespoons fresh parsley chopped
- 2 tablespoons flaxseeds
- 4 tablespoons water
- 4 tablespoon vegan butter

Instructions:

1. Soak flaxseeds in water for 10 minutes
2. Sauté chopped garlic and onion with olive oil in a skillet for 5 minutes.
3. Transfer these veggies to a bowl.
4. Stir in potatoes, flaxseed mixture, and the rest of the ingredients except vegan butter.
5. Mix well, then make 4 patties out of this mixture.
6. Add vegan butter to a skillet and heat it.
7. Sear the patties for about 3-5 minutes per side until golden brown.
8. Serve warm.

Storage Tips:

Pack the uncooked patties in a small ziplock bag or reaction-free container and refrigerate for no more than 3 days or you can freeze them for 3 months. Cook the patties before serving.

The 30-Minute Gluten-free Vegan Cookbook for Beginners
150 simple, delicious, and nutritious whole food, plant-based, and Gluten-free recipes. Make them in under 30 minutes to improve your health and lose weight

183

Cauliflower Bean Dip

Nutritional Values Per Serving	
Calories	245
Total Fat	8.1g
Saturated Fat	1.2g
Cholesterol	0mg
Sodium	36mg
Total Carbohydrate	32.9g
Dietary Fiber	13.8g
Total Sugars	2.4g
Protein	13.3g

 Servings 4

 Preparation Time 15 minutes

 Cooking Time 15 minutes

Ingredients:

- 2 cups cauliflower, cut into florets
- 1 medium garlic clove
- 1 cup cannellini beans, rinsed and drained
- 2 tablespoons tahini
- 1 tablespoon olive oil
- 2 teaspoons lemon juice
- 2 teaspoons lemon zest
- 2 teaspoons fresh thyme
- 1 teaspoon chopped fresh rosemary
- Salt and black pepper to taste

Instructions:

1. Put cauliflower into a steam basket and place it in a steamer over boiling water.
2. Cover and steam the cauliflower for 10 minutes.
3. Blend garlic in a food processor for 1 minute.
4. Add steamed cauliflower and the rest of the ingredients.
5. Blend these ingredients, then serve.

Serving Suggestion:

Serve the bean dip with corn tortilla chips.

Storage Tips:

Keep the dip in a sealable glass container and refrigerate for no more than 3 days.

Zucchini Pasta

 Servings
2

 Preparation Time
15 minutes

 Cooking Time
0 minutes

Nutritional Values Per Serving	
Calories	342
Total Fat	9g
Saturated Fat	1.4g
Cholesterol	0mg
Sodium	976mg
Total Carbohydrate	35.3g
Dietary Fiber	10.3g
Total Sugars	9.7g
Protein	28.3g

Ingredients:

- 2 large zucchini
- 1 cup cherry tomatoes, halved
- 1 cup artichoke hearts, drained and quartered
- ¼ cup diced red onion
- 4 pepperoncini, sliced
- ¼ cup sliced black olives
- ¾ cup cooked chickpeas, drained and rinsed
- ¼ cup vegan Parmesan cheese, shredded

Dressing

- 1 tablespoon olive oil
- 1½ tablespoons red wine vinegar
- 1 tablespoon lemon juice
- ⅛ teaspoon dried basil
- ⅛ teaspoon dried oregano
- ⅛ teaspoon garlic powder
- ⅛ teaspoon fine sea salt
- ¹⁄₁₆ teaspoon black pepper

Instructions:

1. Pass the zucchini through a spiralizer to make zucchini noodles.
2. Mix oil, vinegar, lemon juice, and seasonings in a salad bowl.
3. Toss in zucchini noodles and the rest of the ingredients, then toss well.
4. Serve.

Storage Tips:

Keep this pasta in a sealable storage container and refrigerate for no more than 2 days, or you can freeze the pasta for up to 3 months. Reheat it at medium-low temperature before serving.

The 30-Minute Gluten-free Vegan Cookbook for Beginners
150 simple, delicious, and nutritious whole food, plant-based, and Gluten-free recipes. Make them in under 30 minutes to improve your health and lose weight

185

Chickpea Salad

 Servings
4

 Preparation Time
10 minutes

 Cooking Time
0 minutes

Nutritional Values Per Serving

Calories	309
Total Fat	26.7g
Saturated Fat	7.9g
Cholesterol	25mg
Sodium	639mg
Total Carbohydrate	14.3g
Dietary Fiber	5.3g
Total Sugars	5.3g
Protein	6.7g

Ingredients:

- 3 tablespoons olive oil
- 3 tablespoons lemon juice
- 1 garlic clove, pressed or minced
- ½ teaspoon salt
- ⅛ teaspoon black pepper
- 1 ½ cups cherry tomatoes, halved
- 1 English cucumber, halved and sliced
- 15 ounces chickpeas, drained and rinsed
- ½ red onion, sliced
- 1 avocado, sliced
- ¼ cup cilantro, chopped
- 4 ounces vegan feta cheese, diced

Instructions:

1. Mix oil with lemon juice, garlic, salt, and black pepper in a salad bowl.
2. Toss in the rest of the chickpea salad ingredients and mix well.
3. Serve.

Serving Suggestion:

Enjoy this salad with roasted potatoes.

Storage Tips:

This salad can be best stored in a refrigerator for no more than 2 days or keep it in a freezer for up to 3 months. To do so, pack it in a small ziplock bag or reaction-free container.

Gluten-free Seasoning and Sauces

Teriyaki Sauce

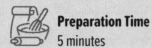 **Servings**
8

 Preparation Time
5 minutes

Cooking Time
0 minutes

Nutritional Values Per Serving	
Calories	48
Total Fat	0g
Saturated Fat	0g
Cholesterol	0mg
Sodium	121mg
Total Carbohydrate	11.4g
Dietary Fiber	0.1g
Total Sugars	10.5g
Protein	0.4g

Ingredients:

- 1 cup gluten-free tamari
- ½ cup apple cider vinegar
- ½ cup pineapple juice
- ½ cup brown sugar
- 1 teaspoon garlic powder

Instructions:

1. Mix vinegar, pineapple juice, and the rest of the ingredients in a 1-quart jar.
2. Cover the lid and shake it to mix well.
3. Serve.

Serving Suggestion:

Use this sauce to season tofu teriyaki or vegetables.

Storage Tips:

Store the sauce in a sealable jar in the refrigerator for up to 2 weeks.

 188

The 30-Minute Gluten-free Vegan Cookbook for Beginners
150 simple, delicious, and nutritious whole food, plant-based, and Gluten-free recipes. Make them in under 30 minutes to improve your health and lose weight

Bechamel Sauce

 Servings 12

 Preparation Time 10 minutes

 Cooking Time 17 minutes

Ingredients:

- 2 ½ tablespoons vegan butter
- 4 tablespoons almond flour
- 4 cups coconut milk
- 2 teaspoons salt
- ¼ teaspoon nutmeg powder

Instructions:

1. Add vegan butter to a suitable saucepan and melt it over medium-low heat.
2. Stir in almond flour, then whisk and cook for 7 minutes until golden brown.
3. Meanwhile, bring coconut milk to a boil in a saucepan, then slowly pour it into the flour mixture while whisking.
4. Add salt and nutmeg, then mix well.
5. Stir well until smooth and simmer for 10 minutes, stirring occasionally.
6. Serve hot.

Serving Suggestion:

Serve this sauce with your favorite entrée.

Storage Tips:

Store the sauce in a sealable jar in the refrigerator for up to 1 week.

The 30-Minute Gluten-free Vegan Cookbook for Beginners
150 simple, delicious, and nutritious whole food, plant-based, and Gluten-free recipes. Make them in under 30 minutes to improve your health and lose weight

189

Hoisin Sauce

Nutritional Values Per Serving	
Calories	28
Total Fat	1.2g
Saturated Fat	0.2g
Cholesterol	0mg
Sodium	66mg
Total Carbohydrate	4.3g
Dietary Fiber	0g
Total Sugars	3.5g
Protein	0.2g

 Servings 12

 Preparation Time 10 minutes

 Cooking Time 0 minutes

Ingredients:

- 1 ½ ounces tamari
- 1 ounce tahini
- 3 teaspoons dark muscovado sugar
- 1 tablespoon white miso paste
- 1 tablespoon toasted sesame oil
- 1 tablespoon blackstrap molasses
- 1 tablespoon water
- 1 teaspoon Chinese five-spice powder
- 1 teaspoon garlic powder

Instructions:

1. Mix tamari and the rest of the ingredients in a 1-quart jar.
2. Cover this jar and shake well to mix.
3. Use as desired.

Serving Suggestion:

Use this sauce to season an Asian meal.

Storage Tips:

Store the sauce in a sealable jar in the refrigerator for up to 2 weeks.

Taco Seasoning

Nutritional Values Per Serving	
Calories	15
Total Fat	0.2g
Saturated Fat	0g
Cholesterol	0mg
Sodium	1220mg
Total Carbohydrate	3g
Dietary Fiber	0.3g
Total Sugars	1g
Protein	0.4g

 Servings
6

 Preparation Time
5 minutes

 Cooking Time
0 minutes

Ingredients:

- 2 tablespoons gluten-free onion powder
- 2 teaspoons gluten-free garlic powder
- 1 tablespoon kosher salt
- 1 tablespoon gluten-free chili powder
- 1½ teaspoons crushed red pepper
- 1½ teaspoons gluten-free ground cumin
- 1 teaspoon dried oregano
- 1½ teaspoons cornstarch
- 1 teaspoon sugar

Instructions:

1. Mix onion powder, garlic powder, and the rest of the ingredients in an 8-ounce jar.
2. Cover with the lid and shake well to mix.
3. Use as desired.

Serving Suggestion:

Use this sauce to season vegetables or tofu.

Storage Tips:

Store the seasoning in a sealable jar in a dry cold place in the kitchen for up to 3 months.

The 30-Minute Gluten-free Vegan Cookbook for Beginners
150 simple, delicious, and nutritious whole food, plant-based, and Gluten-free recipes. Make them in under 30 minutes to improve your health and lose weight

191

Sweet and Sour Sauce

Nutritional Values Per Serving	
Calories	61
Total Fat	0.1g
Saturated Fat	0g
Cholesterol	0mg
Sodium	420mg
Total Carbohydrate	15.7g
Dietary Fiber	0.1g
Total Sugars	13.8g
Protein	0.5g

 Servings 12

 Preparation Time 5 minutes

 Cooking Time 10 minutes

Ingredients:

- 1 cup pineapple juice
- ½ cup chili sauce
- ½ cup maple syrup
- 4 teaspoons rice wine vinegar
- 1½ tablespoons arrowroot starch
- 1 tablespoon water

Instructions:

1. Mix arrowroot starch with water in a bowl.
2. Add pineapple juice, chili sauce, and the rest of the ingredients to a saucepan.
3. Mix well and cook this on a simmer until it thickens.
4. Serve.

Serving Suggestion:

Use this sauce to season vegetables, tofu, etc.

Storage Tips:

Store the sauce in a sealable jar in the refrigerator for 2 weeks.

Cashew Cream Sauce

Nutritional Values Per Serving

Calories	99
Total Fat	8g
Saturated Fat	1.6g
Cholesterol	0mg
Sodium	35mg
Total Carbohydrate	5.7g
Dietary Fiber	0.5g
Total Sugars	0.9g
Protein	2.7g

 Servings 12

 Preparation Time 10 minutes

 Cooking Time 0 minutes

Ingredients:

- 1½ cups raw cashews
- Purified water for soaking
- 1¼ cup purified water for blending
- Juice of ¼ lemon
- 1 dash of sea salt
- 1 tablespoon fresh thyme, chopped

Instructions:

1. Add cashews to a medium bowl and pour in enough water to cover them.
2. Soak the cashews for 12 hours, then drain.
3. Blend the cashews with 1¼ cup water, salt, thyme, and lemon juice in a blender until smooth.
4. Use as required.

Serving Suggestion:

Use this sauce to serve with gluten-free chips or fries.

Storage Tips:

Store the sauce in a sealable jar in the refrigerator for up to 1 week.

The 30-Minute Gluten-free Vegan Cookbook for Beginners
150 simple, delicious, and nutritious whole food, plant-based, and Gluten-free recipes. Make them in under 30 minutes to improve your health and lose weight

193

Dulce De Leche

Servings
12

Preparation Time
15 minutes

Cooking Time
10 minutes

Nutritional Values Per Serving	
Calories	22
Total Fat	1g
Saturated Fat	0.9g
Cholesterol	0mg
Sodium	125mg
Total Carbohydrate	2.8g
Dietary Fiber	0g
Total Sugars	0.1g
Protein	0.3g

Ingredients:

- 1 (10-ounces) can of coconut milk
- ½ cup coconut sugar
- ¼ teaspoon sea salt
- ½ teaspoon vanilla bean
- ½ teaspoon tapioca starch

Instructions:

1. Add canned coconut milk and coconut sugar to a pot and heat over medium heat.
2. Stir in sugar, salt, and vanilla, then mix well.
3. Add the tapioca starch, stir and cook for 10 minutes on a simmer until the mixture thickens.
4. Allow the sauce to cool, then serve.

Serving Suggestion:

Use this sauce to add flavor to gluten-free cakes or desserts.

Storage Tips:

Store the sauce in a sealable jar in the refrigerator for up to 2 weeks.

Roasted Red Pepper Sauce

Nutritional Values Per Serving	
Calories	69
Total Fat	6g
Saturated Fat	3.8g
Cholesterol	0mg
Sodium	14mg
Total Carbohydrate	3.1g
Dietary Fiber	0.7g
Total Sugars	0.4g
Protein	1.3g

 Servings
12

 Preparation Time
10 minutes

 Cooking Time
0 minutes

Ingredients:

- ½ cup jarred roasted red peppers
- ¼ cup smoked almonds
- 1 plum tomato, chopped
- 2 tablespoons red wine vinegar
- 1 garlic clove, chopped
- Pinch of paprika
- ¼ teaspoon crushed red pepper
- ⅓ cup coconut cream
- Salt and black pepper to taste

Instructions:

1. Blend red peppers with nuts, tomato, red vinegar, and the rest of the ingredients in a blender until smooth.
2. Use as required.

Serving Suggestion:

Use this sauce to season your favorite entrée.

Storage Tips:

Store the sauce in a sealable jar in the refrigerator for up to 2 weeks.

The 30-Minute Gluten-free Vegan Cookbook for Beginners
150 simple, delicious, and nutritious whole food, plant-based, and Gluten-free recipes. Make them in under 30 minutes to improve your health and lose weight

195

Walnut Sauce

Nutritional Values Per Serving	
Calories	90
Total Fat	8g
Saturated Fat	2.6g
Cholesterol	0mg
Sodium	4mg
Total Carbohydrate	3.4g
Dietary Fiber	1.6g
Total Sugars	0.6g
Protein	3.1g

 Servings
12

 Preparation Time
10 minutes

 Cooking Time
0 minutes

Ingredients:

- 1 cup walnut halves, toasted
- 2 garlic cloves, minced
- ¼ cup nutritional yeast
- 1 teaspoon dried herbs
- ½ cup almond milk
- Salt and black pepper to taste
- 1 teaspoon lemon juice

Instructions:

1. Blend walnuts with garlic, yeast, and herbs in a food processor until crumbly.
2. Add milk, black pepper, salt, and lemon juice, then blend again for 1 minute.
3. Use as desired.

Serving Suggestion:

Use this sauce to season your favorite entrée.

Storage Tips:

Store the sauce in a sealable jar in the refrigerator for 2 weeks.

Dill Pesto Sauce

Nutritional Values Per Serving	
Calories	92
Total Fat	7.3g
Saturated Fat	1.1g
Cholesterol	0mg
Sodium	33mg
Total Carbohydrate	7g
Dietary Fiber	1.4g
Total Sugars	0.4g
Protein	2.6g

 Servings 12

 Preparation Time 10 minutes

 Cooking Time 0 minutes

Ingredients:

- 2 cups fresh dill
- ½ lemon, juiced
- ½ cup raw cashews
- Salt and black pepper to taste
- 2 garlic cloves, peeled
- 1 medium shallot, diced
- ¼ teaspoon ground cumin
- 1 tablespoon Dijon mustard
- ¼ cup olive oil

Instructions:

1. Blend dill with lemon juice and the rest of the ingredients in a blender until smooth.
2. Use as required.

Serving Suggestion:

Use this sauce to season vegetables or roasted dishes.

Storage Tips:

Store the sauce in a sealable jar in the refrigerator for up to 2 weeks.

The 30-Minute Gluten-free Vegan Cookbook for Beginners
150 simple, delicious, and nutritious whole food, plant-based, and Gluten-free recipes. Make them in under 30 minutes to improve your health and lose weight

197

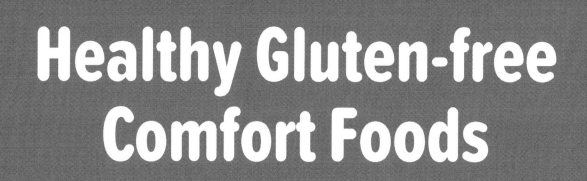

Healthy Gluten-free Comfort Foods

Vegan Cannellini Beans

 Servings 4

 Preparation Time 10 minutes

Cooking Time 15 minutes

Nutritional Values Per Serving	
Calories	352
Total Fat	28g
Saturated Fat	3.7g
Cholesterol	0mg
Sodium	604mg
Total Carbohydrate	26.6g
Dietary Fiber	6.2g
Total Sugars	12.9g
Protein	4.3g

Ingredients:

- 1 tablespoon olive oil
- 1 onion, diced
- 2 cloves garlic, minced
- 2 cans cannellini beans, rinsed
- 2 cans dried tomatoes
- ½ teaspoon salt
- ½ teaspoon black pepper
- 1 ½ teaspoon oregano
- 2 teaspoons Italian seasoning
- Basil, to garnish

Instructions:

1. Sauté onion and garlic with olive oil in a large skillet for 5 minutes.
2. Add tomatoes, beans, salt, black pepper, oregano, and Italian seasoning, then cook for 10 minutes, stirring occasionally.
3. Garnish with basil.
4. Serve.

Serving Suggestion:

Serve with some roasted vegetables.

Storage Tips:

Store the beans in a sealable jar for 2 days in the refrigerator or freezer for 2 months.

The 30-Minute Gluten-free Vegan Cookbook for Beginners
150 simple, delicious, and nutritious whole food, plant-based, and Gluten-free recipes. Make them in under 30 minutes to improve your health and lose weight

199

Sesame Tofu with Veggies

Nutritional Values Per Serving	
Calories	293
Total Fat	3g
Saturated Fat	0.3g
Cholesterol	62mg
Sodium	1040mg
Total Carbohydrate	55.7g
Dietary Fiber	2.1g
Total Sugars	4.7g
Protein	11.3g

 Servings 4

 Preparation Time 15 minutes

Cooking Time 18 minutes

Ingredients:

- 1 lb. block tofu
- 3 tablespoons tamari
- 3 tablespoons rice vinegar
- 2 tablespoons maple syrup
- 1 tablespoon sesame oil
- 1 teaspoon grated ginger

- 1 garlic clove, minced
- 1 bell pepper, diced
- 1 broccoli head, diced
- 1 asparagus, diced
- 1 tablespoon sesame seeds

Instructions:

1. Preheat your oven to 375 degrees F.
2. Mix tamari, rice vinegar, maple syrup, sesame oil, ginger, and garlic in a large bowl.
3. Toss in tofu and mix well to coat. Cover and marinate for 3 minutes.
4. Add veggies to the same bowl and mix well to coat with the marinade.
5. Layer a large sheet pan with a parchment sheet.
6. Spread tofu and all the veggies in the sheet pan, then bake for 15 minutes.
7. Garnish with sesame seeds.
8. Serve.

Storage Tips:

Put the sesame tofu into a container and refrigerate for 2 days or freeze for up to 3 months.

 200

Mexican Quinoa

 Servings
2

 Preparation Time
10 minutes

 Cooking Time
25 minutes

Nutritional Values Per Serving

Calories	417
Total Fat	22.7g
Saturated Fat	8.3g
Cholesterol	0mg
Sodium	1650mg
Total Carbohydrate	49g
Dietary Fiber	5.1g
Total Sugars	7.7g
Protein	9g

Ingredients:

- 1 tablespoon olive oil
- 1 onion, chopped
- 1 red pepper, chopped
- 1 jalapeno pepper, chopped
- 1 (15-ounce) can black beans
- 1 cup corn kernels, canned
- 1 teaspoon chili powder
- ½ teaspoon salt
- 1 cup uncooked quinoa
- 1 cup salsa
- 1 cup vegetable stock
- Cilantro to garnish

Instructions:

1. Sauté onion, red pepper, and jalapeno with olive oil in a large pan for 3 minutes.
2. Stir in beans, chili powder, corn, and salt, then cook for 2 minutes.
3. Add salsa, quinoa, and vegetable stock, and simmer for 20 minutes.
4. Garnish with cilantro.
5. Serve warm.

Storage Tips:

Store the quinoa in a sealed container in the refrigerator for 2 days or freeze for up to 3 months.

The 30-Minute Gluten-free Vegan Cookbook for Beginners
150 simple, delicious, and nutritious whole food, plant-based, and Gluten-free recipes. Make them in under 30 minutes to improve your health and lose weight

201

Chickpea Bolognese Spaghetti Squash

Nutritional Values Per Serving

Calories	529
Total Fat	24.4g
Saturated Fat	4.5g
Cholesterol	7mg
Sodium	2695mg
Total Carbohydrate	69.6g
Dietary Fiber	9.5g
Total Sugars	33.3g
Protein	10.8g

Servings 2

Preparation Time 15 minutes

Cooking Time 15 minutes

Ingredients:

- 1 spaghetti squash, halved crosswise, seeded
- 2 large shallots, diced
- 2 tablespoons olive oil
- 1 teaspoon salt
- ¼ teaspoon black pepper
- 4 garlic cloves, minced
- 24 ounces marinara sauce
- 1 (15-ounce) can of garbanzo beans, drained and rinsed
- ½ cup fresh parsley, chopped

Instructions:

1. Put one cup of water in your Instant Pot and place the steamer basket inside.
2. Add spaghetti squash to the steamer basket, seal the pressure lid and cook on High pressure for 7 minutes.
3. Meanwhile, sauté shallots with olive oil, black pepper, and salt in a skillet for 3 minutes.
4. Stir in garlic, then cook for 1 minute.
5. Add chickpeas and mash them lightly with a spoon, then cook for 1 minute.
6. Stir in marinara sauce, then cook for 3 minutes.
7. Once the squash is done, release the pressure, then remove the lid.
8. Shred the spaghetti squash with a fork and divide the shreds into serving bowls.
9. Top the spaghetti squash with chickpea mixture and garnish with parsley.
10. Serve warm.

Serving Suggestion:

Enjoy the spaghetti squash with cucumber salad.

Storage Tips:

Store the topping and spaghetti squash separately in sealable bowls in the refrigerator and reheat before serving.

Mini Hasselback Potatoes

Nutritional Values Per Serving

Calories	329
Total Fat	8.2g
Saturated Fat	0.9g
Cholesterol	0mg
Sodium	450mg
Total Carbohydrate	62.1g
Dietary Fiber	4.9g
Total Sugars	2.5g
Protein	7.1g

 Servings 4

 Preparation Time 10 minutes

Cooking Time 30 minutes

Ingredients:

Hasselback Potatoes

- 1 ½ pounds of small potatoes
- 2 tablespoons olive oil
- ¾ teaspoon salt
- ¼ teaspoon black pepper

Vegan Aioli

- ⅓ cup vegan, gluten-free mayo
- ⅓ cup olive oil
- 1 ½ tablespoons fresh lemon
- 1 large garlic clove
- ½ teaspoon fine salt
- ¼ teaspoon ground black pepper
- ½ cup fresh Italian flat-leaf parsley
- ½ cup fresh cilantro, chopped

Instructions:

1. Preheat your oven to 450 degrees F.
2. Cut ⅛-inch apart slits on top of each potato.
3. Mix black pepper, salt, and oil and brush this mixture over each potato.
4. Place the hasselback potatoes on a baking sheet and bake them for 30 minutes.
5. To prepare the aioli, mix mayo with the rest of the ingredients in a blender.
6. Pour the aioli over the roasted potatoes and serve.

Serving Suggestion:

Serve these potatoes with roasted carrots or cucumber salad.

Storage Tips:

Keep these potatoes packed in a sealed container and refrigerate for 3 days. Bake them for 5-10 minutes before serving.

The 30-Minute Gluten-free Vegan Cookbook for Beginners
150 simple, delicious, and nutritious whole food, plant-based, and Gluten-free recipes. Make them in under 30 minutes to improve your health and lose weight

203

BBQ Tofu and Vegetables

Nutritional Values Per Serving

Calories	300
Total Fat	17g
Saturated Fat	0.1g
Cholesterol	0mg
Sodium	796mg
Total Carbohydrate	27g
Dietary Fiber	5g
Total Sugars	11g
Protein	14g

 Servings 4

 Preparation Time 20 minutes

Cooking Time 30 minutes

Ingredients:

- 16 oz. firm organic tofu, drained, diced
- 1 small broccoli, cut into florets
- 1 large sweet potato, sliced
- 1 large bell pepper, seeded and sliced
- ⅓ cup BBQ sauce

Dry Rub

- 2 teaspoons smoked paprika
- 2 teaspoons cumin
- 2 teaspoons garlic powder
- 1 teaspoon onion powder
- 1 teaspoon salt
- ½ teaspoon black pepper
- 3 tablespoons avocado oil

Instructions:

1. Preheat your oven to 425 degrees F.
2. Grease a suitable baking sheet with cooking spray.
3. Mix the dry rub ingredients in a bowl.
4. Stir in avocado oil last to make a paste.
5. Add vegetables, BBQ sauce, and tofu, then mix well to coat.
6. Spread the diced tofu and vegetables on a baking sheet and bake for 30 minutes.
7. Serve warm.

Serving Suggestion:

Serve the tofu with veggies with a corn tortilla.

Storage Tips:

Pack the tofu with veggies in a container and refrigerate for up to 2 days or freeze for 3 months.

Sweet Potato Quinoa Tots

 Servings
4

 Preparation Time
20 minutes

 Cooking Time
20 minutes

Nutritional Values Per Serving	
Calories	270
Total Fat	3.8g
Saturated Fat	0.6g
Cholesterol	0mg
Sodium	749mg
Total Carbohydrate	49.5g
Dietary Fiber	6.4g
Total Sugars	3.3g
Protein	9.3g

Ingredients:

- 1 cup cooked quinoa
- ¾ cup oat flour
- 1 cup sweet potato, mashed
- 1¼ teaspoons salt
- ¼ teaspoon black pepper

Instructions:

1. Mix quinoa with oat flour and the rest of the ingredients in a bowl.
2. Make 25 equal-sized tots out of this mixture.
3. Line a baking sheet with parchment paper.
4. Preheat your oven to 400 degrees F.
5. Spread the tots on the baking sheet and bake for 20 minutes.
6. Flip the tots once cooked halfway through.
7. Serve.

Serving Suggestion:

Serve quinoa tots with vegan, gluten-free tomato sauce.

Storage Tips:

Place the uncooked tots in a sealable container and freeze them until ready to cook and serve.

The 30-Minute Gluten-free Vegan Cookbook for Beginners
150 simple, delicious, and nutritious whole food, plant-based, and Gluten-free recipes. Make them in under 30 minutes to improve your health and lose weight

205

Chocolate Avocado Truffles

Nutritional Values Per Serving	
Calories	265
Total Fat	20.5g
Saturated Fat	10.4g
Cholesterol	1mg
Sodium	589mg
Total Carbohydrate	22.4g
Dietary Fiber	5g
Total Sugars	14.5g
Protein	2.2g

 Servings
4

 Preparation Time
25 minutes

 Cooking Time
2 minutes

Ingredients:

Truffles

- 1 cup vegan dark chocolate
- 2 tablespoons unrefined coconut oil
- 1 medium ripe California avocado, pitted and peel removed
- 2 tablespoons unsweetened cocoa powder
- 3 tablespoons pure maple syrup
- 2 teaspoons pure vanilla extract
- ⅛ teaspoon fine salt

Coating

- 1 cup unsweetened shredded coconut

Instructions:

1. Mash avocado flesh in a bowl.
2. Mix dark chocolate and oil in a large microwave-safe bowl.
3. Heat this chocolate in the microwave for 2 minutes on high heat, then mix until melted.
4. Add avocado mash, cocoa, maple syrup, vanilla extract, and salt, then mix evenly.
5. Take a 1½ tbsp. cookie scoop and make equal-sized balls out of the avocado mixture.
6. Roll these balls in the shredded coconut to coat and place them on a baking sheet.
7. Refrigerate them for 15 minutes.
8. Serve.

Storage Tips:

Store the truffles in a sealed container in your refrigerator for 7 days and freeze for up to 6 months.

 206

The 30-Minute Gluten-free Vegan Cookbook for Beginners
150 simple, delicious, and nutritious whole food, plant-based, and Gluten-free recipes. Make them in under 30 minutes to improve your health and lose weight

Zucchini Pizza Bites

Nutritional Values Per Serving	
Calories	273
Total Fat	23.1g
Saturated Fat	5.7g
Cholesterol	16mg
Sodium	349mg
Total Carbohydrate	9.4g
Dietary Fiber	2g
Total Sugars	5.1g
Protein	9.7g

 Servings 4

 Preparation Time 15 minutes

 Cooking Time 7 minutes

Ingredients:

- 1 large zucchini, sliced
- ⅔ cup marinara sauce
- 4 tablespoons vegan mozzarella cheese, shredded
- ⅓ cup olive oil
- Salt and black pepper to taste

Instructions:

1. Preheat your oven to 500 degrees F.
2. Line two baking sheets with parchment paper.
3. Place the zucchini slices on the baking sheets.
4. Drizzle olive oil, black pepper, and salt over the zucchini slices.
5. Divide marinara sauce and vegan mozzarella cheese on top.
6. Bake these slices for 7 minutes.
7. Serve.

Storage Tips:

Store the bites in a sealable jar in the refrigerator for 2 days. Reheat in the microwave for 5 minutes before serving.

The 30-Minute Gluten-free Vegan Cookbook for Beginners
150 simple, delicious, and nutritious whole food, plant-based, and Gluten-free recipes. Make them in under 30 minutes to improve your health and lose weight

207

Pumpkin Cookies

Nutritional Values Per Serving

Calories	314
Total Fat	16.7g
Saturated Fat	6.8g
Cholesterol	0mg
Sodium	211mg
Total Carbohydrate	35.8g
Dietary Fiber	3.8g
Total Sugars	16.2g
Protein	6g

 Servings 6

 Preparation Time 20 minutes

 Cooking Time 12 minutes

Ingredients:

- 1 cup quick-cooking oats
- 1 cup blanched almond flour
- ¼ cup maple sugar
- 3 tablespoons arrowroot powder
- 1 teaspoon pumpkin pie spice
- ½ teaspoon baking soda
- ¼ teaspoon fine salt
- ⅓ cup pumpkin puree
- ⅓ cup maple syrup
- 3 tablespoons coconut oil, melted
- 1 teaspoon vanilla extract

Instructions:

1. Preheat your oven to 350 degrees F.
2. Line half of a baking sheet with parchment paper.
3. Blend oats in a food processor for 30 seconds.
4. Mix the blended oats, almond flour, maple sugar, pumpkin pie spice, arrowroot powder, baking soda, and salt in a bowl.
5. Stir in pumpkin puree, maple syrup, coconut oil, and vanilla extract, then mix well until smooth.
6. Take a 1 ½ tbsp-sized cookie scoop to divide the prepared dough onto the baking sheet to make 14 equal-sized cookies.
7. Bake these cookies for 12 minutes, then allow them to cool.
8. Serve.

Storage Tips:

Store the truffles in a sealed container in your refrigerator for 7 days and freeze for up to 6 months.

The 30-Minute Gluten-free Vegan Cookbook for Beginners
150 simple, delicious, and nutritious whole food, plant-based, and Gluten-free recipes. Make them in under 30 minutes to improve your health and lose weight

Conclusion

In a world packed to the gills with fast and overly processed food, it can be a struggle to find clean, gluten-free, healthy vegan options. With that said, your nutritional needs are very real and so are the consequences of ignoring those needs. When it comes to your health, you cannot rely on inauthentic, unsubstantiated random information on the internet.

This cookbook provides a reliable, well-researched guide for embarking on the important journey of transitioning to a vegan, gluten-free diet. I wanted to create a practical compendium of information, recipes, and advice to make your path easier than my own was.

Now is the time to fight your gluten intolerance. Armed with the knowledge contained within this book, you have the tools you need to bring much-needed relief to your life. There are enough recipes here to create an entire menu of healthy nutritious meals. There's enough information to quell any doubts and illuminate the various support options. So please, go ahead and try these recipes. If you enjoy them, leave a review on Amazon. Doing so will help me spread this resource to the countless others out there suffering the same way you did.

The 30-Minute Gluten-free Vegan Cookbook for Beginners
150 simple, delicious, and nutritious whole food, plant-based, and Gluten-free recipes. Make them in under 30 minutes to improve your health and lose weight

(209)

References

6, K. A., 10, C. N., 9, karen F., and 9, A. F. (2019, May 31). *10 mindset changes since I went vegan.* Vegan Runner Eats. Retrieved June 23, 2022, from https://www.veganrunnereats.com/2640/ten-changes-in-my-mindset/

Bjarnadottir, A. (2021, September 9). *21 common signs of gluten intolerance.* Healthline. Retrieved June 23, 2022, from https://www.healthline.com/nutrition/signs-you-are-gluten-intolerant

Farage, P., and Zandonadi, R. (n.d.). *The Gluten-free diet: Difficulties celiac disease patients have to face daily.* Austin Journal of Nutrition and Food Sciences. Retrieved June 23, 2022, from https://austinpublishinggroup.com/nutrition-food-sciences/fulltext/ajnfs-v2-id1027.php

Getting started on a Gluten-free diet: A step-by-step guide. Gluten Intolerance Group. (2021, November 29). Retrieved June 23, 2022, from https://gluten.org/2019/10/14/getting-started-on-a-Gluten-free-diet/

Gluten: What you don't know might kill you. Dr. Mark Hyman. (2019, November 25). Retrieved June 23, 2022, from https://drhyman.com/blog/2011/03/17/gluten-what-you-dont-know-might-kill-you/

Going vegan and the importance of mindset. brownble. (n.d.). Retrieved June 23, 2022, from https://www.brownbleprograms.com/blog/going-vegan-and-the-importance-of-mindset

How psychology steers your food choices – and what it's like to go vegan. Nest. (2018, March 16). Retrieved June 23, 2022, from https://www.latrobe.edu.au/nest/psychology-steers-food-choices-like-go-vegan/

Is veganism truly good for the planet? A step-by-step analysis. Biofriendly Planet | For a Cooler Environment. (2021, May 24). Retrieved June 23, 2022, from https://biofriendlyplanet.com/eco-friendly-tips/is-veganism-truly-good-for-the-planet-a-step-by-step-analysis/

Jessica Migala Headshot Jessica Migala Reviewed by Dietitian Jessica Ball, M. S. (n.d.). *Starting a Gluten-free diet: A guide for beginners.* EatingWell. Retrieved June 23, 2022, from https://www.eatingwell.com/article/288542/starting-a-Gluten-free-diet-a-guide-for-beginners/

Kiah Connolly, M. D. (2020, November 25). *The science behind gluten intolerance.* Healthy Meal Delivery - Trifecta Nutrition. Retrieved June 23, 2022, from https://www.trifectanutrition.com/health/the-science-behind-gluten-intolerance?hs_amp=true

The psychology of becoming vegan. Go Vegan World. (2019, May 8). Retrieved June 23, 2022, from https://goveganworld.com/psychology-becoming-vegan/#:~:text=Vegans%20see%20animal%20products%20as,that%20we%20do%20not%20need.

Raman, R. (2017, December 12). *Gluten-free diet plan: What to eat, what to avoid.* Healthline. Retrieved June 23, 2022, from https://www.healthline.com/nutrition/Gluten-free-diet

S;, N. K. K. (n.d.). *Veganism, aging and longevity: New insight into Old Concepts.* Current opinion in clinical nutrition and metabolic care. Retrieved June 23, 2022, from https://pubmed.ncbi.nlm.nih.gov/31895244/

Sussex Publishers. (n.d.). *8 surprising psychological facts about vegetarians.* Psychology Today. Retrieved June 23, 2022, from https://www.psychologytoday.com/us/blog/the-asymmetric-brain/202001/8-surprising-psychological-facts-about-vegetarians

Team, D. H. (2021, August 27). *Family history of celiac disease: What to do.* Cleveland Clinic. Retrieved June 23, 2022, from https://health.clevelandclinic.org/have-a-family-member-with-celiac-disease-why-you-might-consider-getting-tested/

WebMD. (n.d.). *What are the complications from celiac disease?* WebMD. Retrieved June 23, 2022, from https://www.webmd.com/digestive-disorders/celiac-disease/celiac-disease-complications

The 30-Minute Gluten-free Vegan Cookbook for Beginners
150 simple, delicious, and nutritious whole food, plant-based, and Gluten-free recipes. Make them in under 30 minutes to improve your health and lose weight

211

Recipe Index

The 30-Minute Gluten-free Vegan Cookbook for Beginners
150 simple, delicious, and nutritious whole food, plant-based, and Gluten-free recipes. Make them in under 30 minutes to improve your health and lose weight

213

Index of Ingredients

A

Agave 106, 167

Allspice 73

Almond butter 64, 68, 70, 80, 95, 128, 130, 145, 152

Almond flour 48, 53, 67, 68, 74, 82, 84, 123, 146, 183, 189, 208

Almond milk 49, 50, 53, 61, 66, 67, 74, 76, 77, 78, 80, 82, 83, 84, 145, 164, 169, 196

Almonds 66, 69, 82, 96, 111, 117, 129, 146, 173, 195

Apple 76, 85, 107, 110, 111, 112, 166, 178

Apple cider vinegar 77, 82, 93, 94, 111, 188

Apple sauce 77

Avocado 89, 100, 104, 110, 114, 117, 134, 136, 137, 138, 139, 141, 163, 186, 206

Avocado oil 67, 110, 204

B

Baby spinach 134, 135, 141

Baking powder 68, 70, 74, 79, 81, 82, 84, 146

Baking soda 70, 74, 77, 81, 84, 208

Bananas 67, 69, 71, 74 75, 80, 83, 144, 161, 169,

Bbq sauce 93, 140, 204,

Bean sprouts 62, 168

Beets 119, 172, 178

Bella mushrooms 181

Black beans 58, 100, 101, 104, 114, 136, 158, 162, 201

Blueberries 69, 76, 83, 84, 167,

Broccoli 50, 90, 96, 105, 115, 200, 204

Brown lentils 91, 99

Brown rice 87, 89, 107

Brown sugar 140, 188

Button mushrooms 94, 139

C

Cabbage 59, 112, 134, 141,

Canned black beans 100, 101, 104, 201,

Cannellini beans 59

Capers 118

Cardamom 68, 174

Carrots 45, 47, 49, 53, 54, 56, 59, 61, 88, 89, 91, 105, 107, 114, 145, 149, 152, 177, 178, 203

Cashew nuts 64, 67, 99, 132, 133, 155, 167, 173, 193, 197

Cauliflower 53, 55, 64, 69, 76, 87, 98, 101, 184

Cauliflower rice 76, 98, 101

Cayenne 56, 60, 87

Celery 47, 51, 53, 54, 61, 64, 88, 98, 118, 137, 138, 172

Cherry tomatoes 185, 186

Chia seeds 71, 78, 121, 164, 178

Chickpeas 72, 87, 92, 102, 127, 134, 137, 138, 163, 180, 181, 185, 186, 202

Chili flakes 45, 55, 124

Chocolate chips 77, 121, 123, 128, 130, 144

Cilantro 57, 62, 87, 91, 99, 100, 101, 104, 106, 113, 119, 137, 158, 168, 180, 186, 201, 203

Cinnamon 68, 71, 73, 74, 75, 76, 79, 81, 83, 85, 87, 93, 113, 114, 126, 130, 146, 173

Cocoa powder 77, 78, 128, 155, 206

Coconut cream 67, 95, 145, 155, 161, 195

Coconut milk 48, 55, 60, 62, 63, 96, 99, 106, 123, 168, 180, 189, 194

Coconut sugar 45, 194

Coconut yogurt 70

Collard leaves 137

Cooked rice 90, 100

Crushed tomatoes 180

Coriander 59, 87, 92, 95, 96, 99, 114, 117, 149, 150, 162, 163, 168

Corn flour/cornstarch 95

Cranberries 112

Cremini mushrooms 139

Cucumber 47, 49, 52, 87, 98, 115, 116, 136, 158, 164, 186, 202

Curry powder 52, 55, 62, 89, 90, 91, 92, 95, 96, 99, 106, 107, 117, 149, 150, 180

D

Dark chocolate 121, 126, 128, 157, 206

Date 125, 166

Dijon mustard 112, 132, 197

Dill 49, 125, 140, 172, 197

Dried basil 45, 185

Dried cranberries 112

Dried oregano 45, 47, 61, 100, 101, 103, 104, 160, 185, 191

Dried tomatoes 160, 199

Dry white wine 181

E

Eggplant 52, 133, 135, 156, 179

The 30-Minute Gluten-free Vegan Cookbook for Beginners
150 simple, delicious, and nutritious whole food, plant-based, and Gluten-free recipes. Make them in under 30 minutes to improve your health and lose weight

F

Flaxseeds   67, 68, 70, 74, 75, 81, 84, 121, 128, 183
Fennel 59, 110, 117
Fennel seeds 174
Frozen blueberries 167
Frozen corn 53, 57, 58
Frozen green peas 62, 88, 96, 171
Frozen mixed veggies 46
Frozen pineapple 148

G

Garam masala 52, 92, 95, 96
Garbanzo beans 202
Garlic   45, 46, 47, 48, 49, 50, 51, 52, 55, 56, 58, 59, 61, 62, 63, 64,
   87, 88, 89, 90, 91, 92, 95, 96, 98, 99, 100, 101, 102, 103, 105,
   106, 111, 114, 115, 116, 118, 119, 122, 132, 139, 145, 156, 162, 163,
   168, 170, 179, 180, 183, 184, 185, 186, 188, 190, 191, 195, 196,
   197, 199, 200, 202, 203, 204
Garlic powder 56, 64, 89, 101, 122, 132, 139, 162, 185, 188, 189,
   190, 191, 204
Garlic salt 57
Ginger 49, 62, 91, 92, 95, 102, 105, 106, 113, 116, 164, 166, 168, 173,
   175, 177, 180, 200
Ginger ground 82, 99
Green bell peppers 58, 107, 182
Green beans 45
Green onions 61, 102
Ground cinnamon 74, 75, 83, 85, 87, 93, 126, 146
Ground coriander 87, 92, 95, 99, 117
Ground cumin 87, 92, 95, 98, 101, 103, 163, 191, 197
Ground flax 74, 81, 84, 121, 128
Ground ginger 82, 99
Ground nutmeg 49, 74, 85
Ground turmeric 87, 95, 166, 168

H

Hemp seeds 69
Hot sauce 93
Hummus 135, 136, 138

K

Kale 45, 48, 110, 111, 122, 133, 147
Ketchup 140

L

Leek 117, 181
Lemon juice 63, 67, 70, 87, 111, 114, 115, 117, 122, 127, 132, 137, 138,
   140, 148, 149, 150, 166, 175, 179, 184, 185, 186, 193, 196, 197
Lemon zest 59, 184
Lime juice 55, 62, 103, 158, 168, 180
Lettuce leaves 104, 115, 139, 163

M

Mango 71, 113, 148, 164
Maple syrup 66, 67, 68, 70, 73, 74, 75, 77, 80, 82, 84, 87, 89, 94,
   103, 111, 116, 121, 126, 128, 129, 130, 133, 141, 146, 152, 155, 161,
   169, 173, 175, 179, 192, 200, 206, 208
Medjool dates 125
Mint 71, 113, 114, 164, 174
Molasses 190

N

Nutmeg 49, 74, 85, 130, 189
Nutritional yeast 45, 61, 64, 72, 127, 132, 133, 196

O

Oat flour 70, 77, 128, 205
Oats 71, 73, 75, 79, 81, 83, 85, 121, 126, 130, 160, 208
Olives 185
Olive oil 47, 48, 51, 52, 54, 56, 57, 59, 63, 73, 90, 92, 96, 98, 100,
   101, 102, 103, 104, 105, 110, 111, 112, 114, 115, 117, 118, 119, 122,
   124, 127, 133, 134, 135, 140, 141, 149, 150, 151, 156, 158, 159,
   163, 168, 169, 170, 171, 172, 179, 181, 183, 184, 185, 186, 197,
   199, 201, 202, 203, 207
Onion powder 64, 89, 100, 101, 140, 191, 204
Oranges and orange juice 102, 119, 169
Orange zest 114, 119
Orange blossom water 113
Orange letnils 47

P

Paprika 56, 57, 58, 61, 87, 88, 93, 98, 100, 101, 140, 162, 163, 195,
   204
Parsley   46, 47, 51, 53, 61, 63, 88, 114, 118, 145, 181, 183, 202, 203
Peaches 163
Peanut butter 75, 76, 121, 126, 144, 157
Peanuts   113, 129, 149, 150, 157
Pecans 73, 110, 114
Pesto   159, 197
Pepitas 60, 110

The 30-Minute Gluten-free Vegan Cookbook for Beginners
150 simple, delicious, and nutritious whole food, plant-based, and Gluten-free recipes. Make them in under 30 minutes to improve your health and lose weight

215

Made in United States
Troutdale, OR
11/16/2024

24923438R00122